THE DIARIUM OF MAGISTER

JOHANNES KELPIUS

METALMARK BOOKS

JOHANNES KELPIUS.

FROM THE ORIGINAL CANVAS BY DR. CHRISTOPHER WITT, NOW IN THE HISTORICAL SOCIETY OF PENNSYLVANIA.

The Diarium

of

Magister Johannes Kelpius

WITH ANNOTATIONS BY

JULIUS FRIEDRICH SACHSE

PART XXVII OF A NARRATIVE AND CRITICAL HISTORY
PUBLISHED BY
THE PENNSYLVANIA-GERMAN SOCIETY

LANCASTER, PA.
1917

PRESS OF
THE NEW ERA PRINTING COMPANY
LANCASTER, PA.

I.

THE JOURNAL OF KELPIUS.

Magister Johannes Kelpius, the leader of the band of German Pietists who came to these shores in the year of grace 1694, and settled on the banks of the Wissahickon, will always remain one of the most picturesque characters of our early Pennsylvania-German history; the more so on account of a certain air of mystery and romance which has thus far enshrouded his personality.[1]

Kelpius and his company of German Pietists located

[1] For a full account of Kelpius, see "The German Pietists of Provincial Pennsylvania," Philadelphia, 1895, pp. 219–250.

themselves in what was then unbroken wilderness upon the hills overlooking the Wissahickon Creek, a small stream which winds its way through rocky forest dells and valleys until it mingles its crystal waters with the Schuylkill River.

Changing the scene to the present day, the wilderness where Kelpius and his followers located in the last decade of the seventeenth century, and erected their tabernacle, is now a built-up part of the city of Philadelphia, known as the twenty-first ward, while the Wissahickon with its romantic dells, valleys and rugged hills is now a part of Philadelphia's great natural pleasure ground, known far and wide as Fairmount Park.

Unfortunately Kelpius, in his modesty, left but little written record of the great work performed by him during the fourteen long years that he lived on the banks of the romantic Wissahickon. How earnestly he sought to improve the morals and spiritual condition of the rude and heterogeneous population that was then scattered through eastern Pennsylvania, is shown by the many traditions and legends that have survived for two centuries.

By reason of his scholarly attainments, devout life, independent bearing, and, it may be said, broad humanity, together with his repeated refusals of worldly honors and civil power, that were at various times thrust upon him, the magister on the Wissahickon stands out in bold relief as a prominent example of piety and disinterestedness.

There can be but little doubt that this devout scholar, who thus voluntarily banished himself from the fatherland home and friends had many difficulties to contend with, both within and without the community, and that his position at the head of such a fraternity was anything but a sinecure. There were conflicting interests to equalize and,

J. N. J

The Lamenting Voice
of the
Hidden Love,
at the time
when she lay in Misery & forsaken;
and oprest by the multitude
of Her Enemies
Composed by one
In Kumber.

Mich. VII 8 9. 10

Rejoyce not against me C mine Enemy: when I fall, I shall arise; when I sit in darkness, the Lord shall be a light unto me. I will bear the indignation of the LORD, because I have sinned against him until he plead my cause, & execute judgment for me: he will bring me forth to the light, & I shall behold his righteousness. Then She that is mine enemy shall see it, and shame shall cover her which said unto me, Where is the LORD thy God? mine eyes shall behold her: now shall she be trodden down as the mire of the streets.

Hester signifies Secret, or Hidden, & Haman, multitude of troubles

---

Pennsylvania in America 1705

B. That Cumber is, here above, spel'd with a K, & not with a C, has its peculiar Reason.

ENGLISH TITLE PAGE TO KELPIUS' MS. HYMN BOOK.

upon more than one occasion, stubborn minds to combat. When internal dissensions threatened the fraternity it was always left to Kelpius to use the olive branch.

So far as known to the present writer, but two manuscript volumes of Magister Kelpius have come down to us;

FAC-SIMILE OF TITLE PAGE OF THE KELPIUS JOURNAL.

one a volume of hymns and music,[2] the other, which is the subject of this paper, is his journal or *diarium* in Latin with its daily entries during the voyage from London to Pennsylvania. This commences on the first day of January, 1694, and ends on June 24, the passage having taken ten weeks, the actual voyage starting on the seventh day of February. He divides his entries into six periods and

---

[2] *Ibid.,* pp. 234–243.

three weeks, which covers seventeen pages of the journal; after the following introduction, which is apparently a quotation from Seneca, is headed:

FAC-SIMILE OF INTRODUCTION.

(**Translation.**)

"SENECA DE REFOR."

" I cannot go beyond my country: it is the one of all; no one can be banished outside of this. My country is not forbidden to me, but only a locality. Into whatever land I come, I come into my own: none is exile, but only another country. My country is wherever it is well; for if one is wise he is a traveller; if foolish an exile. The great principle of virtue is, as he said, a mind gradually trained first to barter visible and transitory things, that it may afterwards be able to give them up. He is delicate to whom his country is sweet; but he is strong to whom every single thing is his country; indeed he is perfect to whom the world is exile."

The next leaf may be called a title, and sets forth that the following are "Literal copies of letters to friends in and out of Pennsylvania, sent from the wilderness by Johanno Kelpio, Transylvania, 1694–1703, 4, 5, 6, 7."

THE GOOD SHIP "SARA MARIA," CAPT. TANNER, MASTER.
(*Sara Mariabonae Spei.* Kelpius.)

𝕵. 𝕹. 𝕵.

(In the Name of Jesus)

A. D. 1694.

ON the 7th of Jan., I, convinced by God, resolved upon going to America, my companions being: Henry Bernard Cöster,[11] Daniel Falkner,[12] Daniel Lutke, John Seelig, Ludwig Bidermann,[13] as well as about 40 other companions, some of whom were numbered (mustered), and others convicted by God, in Germany, had as yet in the preceding year, resolved upon that voyage.

On Feb. 7th I engaged for them the ship, " SARAH MARIA," of good hope, Captain John Tanner, an Englishman, the vessel being hired at seven (7) English £ of Silver, which I paid out on board

---

[11] Henrich Bernhard Koster (Coster-Kuster). For full account of this early pioneer and Evangelist cf. " German Pietists in Provincial Pennsylvania," pp. 251–298.

[12] Daniel Falckner. *Ibid.*, pp. 299–334.

[13] Ludwig Christian Biederman was the first member of the community to break his voluntary resolution of celibacy. Almost immediately upon his arrival in Germantown he married Maria Margaretha, the daughter of the widow of Rev. Johann Jacob Zimmermann. *Cf.* " German Pietists," pp. 460–472. They had been fellow passengers across the ocean.

FACSIMILE OF FIRST PAGE OF DIARIUM OF MAGISTER JOHANNES KELPIUS.

the ship on the 14th of this month, having embarked on the 13th, but the rest had embarked on the 12th. 〕

This first day was passed tranquilly on the Thames river, by our people, by me (in this manner) for the greatest part. At nightfall a dispute arose concerning the arrangement of the beds, which (dispute) kindled the zeal in P. G. (puellis, Germanis—German girls?), so that disappointed in the pacific union of heart, I deemed my zeal for obtaining a single bed the heaven of Christ, (zelum and coelum, being here a je de mots). The lewdness might have increased (?) until Maria (solitaria, a spinster, lone woman) brought in an Ethiopian virgin, who would previously inform herself concerning the purity of an European maiden, before she consented to marriage. But George was afflicted with a most severe illness, the condition forbids me here, enough, wherefore in this manner he slept alone.

The second day 4. 15th Feb. was lucky for us (secunda and secunde—2nd & lucky, another je de mots). But the third was destined fatal. My apprehensive mind presaged evils with a fortunate outcome. Falkner said the same of himself. We were visited first by the impress-gang of the king. Then we were driven towards sand-banks[14] by a contrary and turbulent wind; wishing to escape these, we sought safety in our anchor, whereby we should have perished if not Divine providence had made it, that the great weight of the metal, which, under our ship, would have perforated the same had not the anchor been broken itself. Our anchor being lost in this manner, we were at length borne upon the sand-banks by the whirl. All, saving a few, feared the end was at hand. The Captain having fired off four cannon, called those who were near to the rescue, but took pity on none of us. We furled the sails and committed the vessel to the turbulent billows, whilst the sailors were despairing. I had hold (of) the turtle-dove, that is not to be deserted, about the middle (waist) from the begin-

(𝔓age 2 of 𝔐𝔰.)

ning (Feb. 16) of the storm, a divine witness, when already I saw

---

[14] Probably one of the shoals known as the Goodwin Sands.

our pilot despairing in the midst of our distress, when I was admonished, likewise, that by bearing witness concerning the most certain aid of God, I should raise his faith and hope, but being agitated myself, I kept my thoughts for myself. I was admonished a second time, but seeing him intent on other matters and turned away from me, I held my peace in turn. All were despairing and invoked the name of Jesus, as if about to journey into another life. Then being admonished (divinely) for the third time, I said to the pilot: " Have faith in God, who certainly will save us." The pilot rejoiced, for he was not so ignorant of divine matters. He pressed my hands and said: " God alone can help me everywhere, on Him shall I hope." Said, done (No sooner had he said these words than they were fulfilled). The storm began to drive the ship away from the sand-banks into deep water, where casting anchor, we praised God in safety. Meanwhile Cöster, with the rest, had been pouring forth strong supplication to God (and indeed, about that time, when I began to collect my thoughts) as soon as I was admonished for the 3rd time, inwardly, and addressed the pilot, he had changed his entreaty to a prayer of thanksgiving, being sure his wish had been granted, though not knowing what just now was being done by us (with us).

I went below, rejoicing in our deliverance, to announce the glad tidings. I told them what had been done by me just a little while ago, and they, in turn, related their experience; therefore I no longer wondered at the divine virtue in me while I prayed, (their prayers had so powerfully aided me). I went up on deck and explained the matter more fully to the pilot, who began to praise the Lord with folded hands, especially when I added, *that still more dangers were imminent (threatening), but that I was fully convinced of the final aid of God.* Going below for the 2nd time, I also disclosed this matter to my brethren, when Falkner, filled with the spirit of God, poured forth fervent thanksgiving: Praised be the name of the Lord for ever! Amen!. Hallelujah!

HENRICH BERNHARD KÖSTER.
ONE OF THE LEADERS OF THE KELPIUS COMMUNITY ON THE WISSAHICKON.

(page 3 of Ms.)

The fourth day the Sabbath was, indeed, a Sabbath for us, who, in this quietude, persevered in the praises of God, our Preserver.

The fifth day, which was of the sun (*lis-solis?*) the infant son of Henry Lorentz, died, aged 6 months, his remains were cast into the sea (or, "he fell into the sea"). We were again visited by the royal impress gang, who would have borne off as their booty three of the best attendants of our pilot (captain) under pretense of the Swedish nation (for Swedes they were) had not divine favor won over unto us the hearts of the soldiers; for Cöster had previously poured forth a most fervent prayer. By the aforesaid providence, those impressors carried off from a neighboring vessel, that was going to sail to America with us, three Belgian sailors. Thereafter we were happily borne by a gentle breeze from out of that dangerous place to one more secure, and there, having cast anchor, we remained through the night.

On the 6th day, we vainly sought for our lost anchor, but, a great calm arising, we were obliged to rest, making up for the delay by reading the Bible and dissertations on sacred subjects. At night we were in turn visited by the impress-gang, who carried off one of our younger servants, yet we, in turn, acquired a former servant and sailor of the king's.

On the 7th day, we were borne by a favorable wind over (past) rocky and sandy ledges and on the right, leaving behind for ever the shore of England. About even-tide there approached to us some men-of-war with 22 other vessels, bearing and accompanying Prince Ludwig of Baden from England to Holland. At night, casting anchor beyond the rocks, we slept securely and soundly (on either ear).

The 8th day (i. e. the 7th of our sailing), brought Sabbath and rest, for, happily, a south-wind blowing, we were borne to a place called "Downs" by the English, where the rest of the ships that were going to sail to America with us, were assembled.

(PERIOD SECOND)

February At that port (Downs)[15] we awaited for about 2 weeks for a favorable wind, and the royal mandate, shortening the long, weary hours by dissertations on sacred subjects and by study of the Bible. Meanwhile we sent letters to London and to Germany to Tob. Ad. Lauterbach[16] (Feb. 27th) also to others from whom we received answers full of most auspicious omens.[17] The other part (of our company) which had been excluded, at London, on account of their depraved manners, from us and our spiritual intercourse, wasting their time in brawls and fights, were a scandal even to the lower (inferior) sailors, who wondered that the young women were beaten by the men. But even the triumvirate itself (for 3 families had been excluded) was split up into factions, and had not one yielded to another, the matter might have come from words to blows, as I have said was done at the former fight.

March On March 3rd our Captain received another anchor, like unto the one that was lost, though inferior to the latter, yet most acceptable unto us. Scarcely had we received this anchor when we were again visited by a furious storm, and what increased the danger, the two anchors, which we had cast, became interlocked and could hardly be adjusted (set aright) though it took a long time. Loosed, we were, meanwhile being borne nearer and nearer to the rocky and sandy ledges. We saw the cables sustaining the anchor of a ship not far off being torn asunder. We heard the boom of cannon of vessels in despair; at the same time we saw broken spars floating here and there. But what our fate would have been, I could not (was not allowed to) inquire, nevertheless we were extricated out of this danger, we were freed.

---

[15] "The Downs," a spacious roadstead in the English Channel affording an excellent anchorage. It is between the shore and the Goodwin Sands and is much used by the British Navy.

[16] Tob. Ad. Lauterbach, one of the leaders of the Philadelphiac Community.

[17] This was during the universal war then waged against Louis XIV of France, 1689–1697. In American history it is known as "King William's War."

(**Page 5 of Ms.**)

On the following day I received a letter from Samuel Walden-
field, residing in the "Lamp" on Frenchurch St., London, in   March
which letter some money was assigned to me (a draft), sent from   Divine
Holland by a devout (Lat. divina) virgin, Catharine Beerens,   Virgin
van Boswig, said money to be received of Samuel Standeriwk, at
Deal,[18] who received me and my companion Seelig, very civilly, on
the following day, and by way of conversation, he manifested great
interest (was wonderfully delighted) in the affairs of the Pietists
of Germany, and desired that we should often come to see him;
but our unexpected departure on March 8th, frustrated our intention. For the man-of-war accompanying us, received orders   8
from the King to set sail. Therefore, unfurling our sails, about   4
sunset, we were borne along by the east wind with 19 accompanying vessels, whereof 3 were men-of-war.

Next day our Captain received instructions, from the admiral of
the war-vessels, concerning his course of action on the voyage, by   9. ♀
day and by night, in all events, in calm or storm, in peace or war.
They read as follows:—

"Instructions for your (the) Boat or keeping Company with
"their Majesty's Ship ye "Sandados Prize," under my Com-
"mand:—

"If I weigh in ye day I will hauld from my foartop sail shrouds
"and fire a Gunn. If in ye night I will putt a Light in ye main
"topmast shrouds and fire a Gunn, which Light you are to
"answer. If I weigh in fog I will fire 3 guns distinctly one after
"another.

"If I anchor in ye night or in a fogg I will fire 2 Guns a small
"distance of time one from ye other and putt aboard a Light
"more than my constant Lights which Light you are to answer."

(**Page 6 of Ms.**)

"If i lye by or try in the Night, i will fire five Guns, and   March
"keep a Light abroad more than my constant light in the Main-
"Schrouds, and if through extremity of Weather we are forced to

---

[18] Deal, a seaport and market town in Kent, England. It has no harbor.

"lye a Holl or under a Mizon, i will fire three Guns, and put
"abroad two Lights of equal height more than my constant Light,
"and if i make sail in the Night after blowing Weather, or after
"lying by, or for any other reason, i will make the same sign as
"for weighing in the Night, wich Light you are to answer.

"In case of separation if we meet by day, the weathermost ship
"schall lower his Fore-Top-Sail, and those the Levard schall an-
"swer by Lowering their Main-Top-Sail.

"He that apprehends any danger in the Night schall fire Guns
"and put abroad Three Lights of equal height, and bear away, or
"Tack from it; but if it schould happen to be strange ships, then
"make false fires and endeavour to to speack with my (me); and
"to better to Ruon each other in the night, he that hails schall
"ask what schip is that, and he that is heilet schall answer Adven-
"ture, than he that hailet first schall reply Rupert.

(𝕻𝖆𝖌𝖊 7 𝖔𝖋 𝕸𝖘.)

"If i have a desire to speak with you, i will hoist a Jack-Flag
"in my Mizon-Top-Mast-Schrouds, and make a Weft with my
"ensign.

"If you have a desire to speak with my, you schall hoist your
"Ensign in your Pain-Top-Mast-Schrouds.

"If in the night you chance to spring a Leak, keep firing of
"Guns, and showing of Lights."

"Dated on Board their   Will Allen.
"Majesty's Ship "Sandados Prize"
"March ye 9, 169¾.

On the third day we were borne by a favorable wind, leaving,
at about noon, the Isle of Wight on the right. On the 4th day,
which was a Sunday, with bright sunshine, a most gentle, yet very
favorable breeze blowing, we entered the harbor of Plymouth (than
which we could have scarcely wished a better) about five o'clock
in the evening, and lo! the Belgian war-ships, ceding, as it were,
their station unto us, left the port. We, entering port, occupied
their former place, & now safely moored from billows and storms,
we had, moreover, to the west, our men-of-war, & a citadel, con-

If i have a desire to speak with you, Hos
i will hoist à Jack-Flag in my mizon-
Top-Mast-Shrouds, and make à Weft
with my ensign.

If you have a desire to speak with
my, you schall hoist your ~~Fore~~ Ensign in
your Main-Top-Mast-Shrouds.

If in the Night you ~~change~~ chance
to spring a Leak, keep-firing of Guns, and
showing of Lights.

Dated on Board this   Witt. Allen
Maj:s Ship Sandades Prize
March y.e 9. 169 ¾

Tertia die secundo vento ferebamur relin-   1a
quentes circa meridiem à dextris insulam Wight   5

Lic latitudo Solis erat sole serenissimo, vento   11r
benissimo sic tamen severico maxime, qui meliorem nobis   E
exoptare vix potuissemus. intrabantusiap ortum Plymu-
thianum circa horam quintam vespertinam, stieux
naves Belgicæ bellicæ nobis quasi locum cedentes gre-
dientes ante portum obinam faciebant in grooti
locum nos ingredientes optimum occupa baunus alli-
gantes navim rupibus Et proram anhora firmas-
Ete post extra omnes fluctuum Et procellarum
injurias habentes insuper ante nos ex Belgich naves
Bellicæ Et arcem totidem, quot Anni dies nempe
trecenta et sexagenta quinty tormenta continentem

taining as many guns (cannon) as there are days in the year, namely 365.

(𝔓𝔞𝔤𝔢 8 𝔬𝔣 𝔐𝔰.)

PERIOD THIRD.

At this place we tarried for five weeks, vainly expecting the royal convoys. Meanwhile we became familiar with sundry citizens of Plymouth. The rest of our time was spent in sacred exercises & meditation. I, for my part, received some letters from Cleves & Nüremberg, wherefore I was not so much in a quandary concerning the manner of our voyage, but I answered all objections satisfactorily, directing moreover other letters to Lauterbach, Mons de Wateville, Moerkamp & others, chiefly at London.

April 15

But when, on April 15th, Danish, Swedish & Spanish floats landed, we bargained with these for their convoy,[19] & gave up waiting for the royal vessels, & on the 18th, with a favorable south

18.8 +

wind, the sea being clear, we ventured on our voyage, at about 10 a.m. But, lo! when we had scarcely left port, we were driven about by a contrary breeze, moreover, we descried three stately ships, which we first took to be French men-of-war, but found out afterwards they were Portuguese. During the night a heavy fog arose, so that we were borne along, as it were, blind-folded & lost the English coast, to which, resplendent in the evening sun, we had bidden farewell, directing our course westward with a favoring north-wind, & with 38 vessels accompanying, being mostly Spanish, these first discoverers but now hated settlers of the new world, conveying us, seemingly, towards a better hope.

On this day, on account of the opposition of ☉ & ♄ 20. ♀ the superstitious crew expected a huge tempest, but an altogether indifferent sky permitted a prosperous course under Lat. 49° 33'. At the same time also on the following days ♄ & ☉ & so that that formidable opposition neither from before nor behind exercised (?) their powers.

---

[19] In this war, under the league of Augsburg, almost the whole of Europe was arrayed against France.

(𝔓age 9 of 𝔐s.)

On this day the south wind blew rather violently. Hourly we April
traversed 5 English miles, but our convoys were scattered all day 23. ☽
long & could hardly be kept together by their highest officers. At
mid-day the wind veered from south to west, scarcely giving us
time for furling sail, & awaiting, as yet, the dispersed vessels, our
main-mast sail alone expanded, we ploughed leisurely, the hostile
sea. So the most favorable aspect of the constellations had caused
one of the worst storms.

Hereafter, on the 24th, under Lat. 48° 9′, our ships were 24. ♀
gathered together. On the 25th, under Lat. 47° 49′, with a favor- 25.8
able east-wind, we bade farewell, in the evening, to our Spanish +
convoys, rewarding them also. The name of their highest officer
was Nicholas De Rudder.

PERIOD FOURTH.

Leaving, therefore, the Spanish vessels 25-behind, we were May
borne from Lat. 47° 3′ to Lat. 43° 58′, being favoured by a most
delightful east-wind throughout the week. In longitude we traversed more than 300 leagues (1200 geog. mi.), so prosperous was
the 2nd week of our voyage. But on the 1st day of the 3rd week, 2.8
which was the 2nd of May, there blew an ugly west-wind, which +
sorely vexed us on the following night.

(𝔓age 10 of 𝔐s.)

3. An auspicious day. A north-wind drove us from our place. 3. ♃
4. In consequence of the wind changing to west, we were tossed May
about all night, being hurried along on the tempestuous gale. At 4. ♀
the 3rd night-watch it veered towards the north. 5. Weathering 4.5.
fierce storms, we finally proceeded with a favorable north-wind. 6. ☉.
6. Under Lat. 49° 55′, with west-wind, we sailed southward, until,
at last, on the 7th, we passed through an unfavorable night. Dur- 7. ☽
ing the day, we encountered several storms, losing our fore-masts,
that of the prow & 2 of the middle (the twin masts). Moreover,
we were unable to ascertain our latitude, neither moon, sun, nor

2

8. ♂   stars appearing; but a little before evening devotions, a north-wind cheered the sailors. 8. Under Lat. 41° 22', we sailed along happily, restoring, in part, our lost masts.

PERIOD FIFTH.

9.8
    +

10. ♃

May

Our stormy week being at an end, we entered upon a warlike one. Scarcely had we arisen after a turbulent night, when squalls prevented our refitting the masts. Early on the 10th, we beheld from afar, three vessels. Presently they advanced toward us. Some conjectured they were English ships homeward bound from American shores. But when, after hoisting our colors, we perceived, they did not reply, but kept on approaching nearer and nearer, we thought, they were bent on an engagement. In this we erred not. For they were French, & their largest vessel carried 22 cannon, the 2nd 10, & the smallest 6 cannon, & since they sailed with a favorable wind, they challenged us to battle. We, having made preparations for ½ an hour, kept on the defensive only, & that so bravely,

(Page 11 of Ms.)

that the largest vessel took to flight. Our companion vessel the "Providence," seeing this, came up to us, already victors, to the pursuit of the French vessels, which, now, all fled with every sail expanded. And because the "Providence" was of superior speed, she alone coped with the fleeing vessels, with such eagerness, as though we had gained a greater victory. Sometimes, however, whilst being greatly troubled by her three adversaries, she would wait for us to come up, until, at last, we obtained possession of the smallest ship, which carried six cannon. With this we were contented, although we could have captured the rest, yet, deeming that superfluous, we began to sing a song of triumph (paean).

Strange to say, in this battle of four hours' duration, we were struck by three cannon-balls only, & that without any one's being hurt, & with but little damage to our vessel. On board the vessel we captured, one man had been wounded in his foot, another had his head torn off, & the remaining ships, what losses had they not sustained? On this and on the following day, we, marvelling at

divine Providence, worshipped & praised the name of God. But 11. ♀
marry, the vicissitudes of human affairs! Again two vessels loomed
up, are they friends or foes? We were in a quandary. We also
recollected, that two French war-ships were still at large, & we
had heard our prisoners remark, that one of those carried 80 cannon, & the other was an armored one. Hence we again prepared
ourselves for another encounter. They however, altered their May

(page 12 of Ms.)

course & thus, what seemed to be our ruin, came happily off, & we,
our fears being somewhat allayed, rested our weary limbs.

Occasionally, we were amused by the gambols of the monsters
of the deep, some having the form of calves, others that of horses,
and still others that of whales. Especially at night they presented
a fine spectacle, when vying, as it were, in speed with our vessel,
they seemed just as moving through a sea of fire, (Phosphores-
cence). But, lo! ·/2. Late in the morning another ship hove in 12. ♄.
sight, just as if six navigators had met, first three to two, then two
to three (——for we were sailing already with our booty), lastly,
one being offered to our view. Concerning this last vessel, our
minds were uneasy but for short space, since no sooner had she
appeared, than she withdrew. The French vessels returning from
Martinique had thus far troubled us enough.

Sunday, bright sun-shine, under Lat. 39° 48′, laying care aside, 13. ♉. 13.
we were cheered by a favorable east-wind; shortly before, it had
been from the north. Then with heavy sea-weed (?), we ploughed 14. ☽
the main. On the 15th, the wind veering to south, we slacked
our course, meanwhile the sailors looked with covetous eyes at our
French prey, grumbling at our captain, who kept appeasing his
hunger for sugar, & quenching his thirst for cider (with which
merchandise the ship was fraught), until he promised that all
should be partakers, just as himself, of the unjust mammon, as
soon as the latter should have been made of private right from (by)
the lawful judges of these matters (pilfered from them).

PERIOD SIXTH.

(**Page 13 of Ms.**)

May
16. 17.
8. ♃·
+

18. ♀

19.5.

20. ☉

21. ☽
22. ♂ He
was Peter
Blessed.

23.
8
+

May
24.

The fifth week of the warfare, the 16th day began under Lat. 39° 21', the 17th, morn advanced, presented a ship returning from Antego, though first preparing for battle with the same, yet we spent the remainder of the day most amicably, & entrusted letters for London with the same, determining (settling) also the controversy (dispute) concerning our French booty, from which we had taken two cannon. On the 18th, east wind shortly before midnight winged our flight, but scarcely four sails were unfurled on account of the lazy-tardy bulk of our French prey. We tarried, therefore, for the latter, & on the 19th, tired of waiting, we bade farewell to the " Providence," leaving her in charge of the booty, & so we went (proceeded) before alone, leaving all the ships behind, that had set out with us from England. But on the 20th, the wind being contrary and exceedingly strong, which hardly moderated on the 21st & 22nd. At this juncture, I recalled a Prophet, x who prophesied for me x while yet in London, that Cherubim would be the companion of our way & our protectors in danger, & that this would be a sign that we should accept of Divine assistance, to wit, that although having left behind all other vessels, yet we alone should precede with contrary wind, & should happily draw (come) ashore in America, i. e. 23. The sixth week, looking at our companions, you would say, they are snugly at Philadelphia, they were borne in love. North-wind also seemed to favor, but, as if heaven had decreed otherwise, a west-wind visited us with storms, when already in Lat. 37°, we were approaching Virginia, which we sought. Therefore on the 25th, we were driven northward to Lat. 39°, whilst the sailors were becoming apprehensive, for a huge

(**Page 14 of Ms.**)

4. ♀
25.
26. ♄

o

vessel seemed to sail by, (Flying Dutchman?). But on the 26th, late in the morning, we came, very unexpectedly, up to seven ships. These were returning from Virginia to England. To our great dismay we learned from them, that we were as yet 250 leagues distant from land——most agreeably to our reckoning. We entrusted

unto them letters to London, & bade farewell & directed our course
from Circins (?) to Notolybinn (?). Which line, also, we fol-
lowed on the 27th, the blessed day of Pentecost (Whit-Sunday) &
on the 28th & 29th. The seventh week was the most steadfast in
inconstancy, for now we were borne south, now north. But on the
31st, the wind turned from Circins (?) to north, presently to
Caecins, (north-east) then to east to Libanotus, and lastly, to south-
west. June 1st, just as yesterday, we experienced variable wind,
but yesterday it was clear, to-day, however, we had rain-storms
(showers), & about eventide we were cherished (comforted) by a
huge parasite fish (Shirk), at the same time a strong north-east
wind steadily kept advancing us about two leagues per hour
throughout the entire night. The same north-east wind, though
less constant, favored us. During the morning hours, a dolphin of
medium size was caught in our (unmoved) anchor. He was yellow
as gold, spotted with red.

29. ☉
28. ☽
29. ♂
30. ☿
  +
31. ♃

June
1. ♀

2. ♄

June

(𝔓𝔞𝔤𝔢 15 𝔬𝔣 𝔐𝔰.)

(The dolphins must have been wedged between anchor & poop!)
(When (while) from the opposite, our parasite of yesterday, with
huge bulk, & seven foot length tickled neither our eyes so much, nor
our taste yet the dolphin filled out both, though not confirming
credibility (stapability) the fable of the ancients concerning the love
of music, unless, perchance, you should say our English crew erred
in the name.   3. To-day an uninterrupted & brisk north-east wind
drove us directly away from a ship we should otherwise have met.
Whether the latter were friend or foe, we could not tell. Nevertheless they seemed to entertain some fear & sailed back, whence they
had come.   4. Under lat. 38° 10′ we had favorable north-east,
soon after changing to east, then to south-east under lat. 36° 53′,
where with full sail, we outstripped the birds, so that on the following 5th & 6th, on the completion of our seventh week, we augured,
we should see dry land; nor should we have been deceived in our
augury, had not the wind changed from south to south-west.

4. 7. & 8. & 9.   The same south-west wind continuing, we were
driven north-east-ward, & disappointed in our hope of descrying

June

3. ☉

4. ☽

5. ♂
6. ☿
  +
7. 8. 9.

land. 10. ☉ But yet, on the 50th day after our departure from
10. ☉ England, we touched the bottom of the sea at only 38 threads
(fathoms? 38 × 6 = — 228 feet).

But lo! for four hours we were tossed about by a double storm
& wind until,

June
(𝔓𝔞𝔤𝔢 16 𝔬𝔣 𝔐𝔰.)

11. ☽ at last, north-east wind, so often longed for, favored us, which,
12. ♂ nevertheless, on the 11th, turned to north, so that, although almost entering port, yet we could not accomplish this end. 12.
From afar we descried three vessels, & from about 8½ a.m. to 12
noon, we beheld a huge eclipse of the sun under lat. 36° 45'.
And lo! the eclipse over, we entered by a most blessed influence
(considering externalities) the bay of Virginia (Chesapeake) towards 8 p.m., casting anchor somewhat after midnight.

Ninth Week

8. 13
+
4. 14   Beginning with the new & ninth week, a good south-west blowing, we traversed 40 leagues, until, leaving the coast of Virginia
15. 16   & sailing along that of Maryland, we went to the lord-protectors
royal deputies (procurators region) to inform them of the why &
wherefore of our coming to the new world. Having tasted of the
fruits, which grew in great abundance along the shore, we pursued the remainder of our way.

*The memorable excommunication of Falkner by Cöster, & that
of Anna Maria Schuchart, the Prophetess of Erfurt (Erphorti-
anae)!*

Tenth Week

In the tenth week. 19. we all went ashore (disembarked),
(literally "kissed the ground (earth")) 5. 22. Went to New
Castle; 23 ☉ to Philadelphia, & finally 24. ☽ to Germantown.

Then follow copies of the nine missives sent to persons
at home and abroad, viz.:

---

[3] Henrich Johann Deichman, leader of the Philadelphiac Movement in Europe.

[4] Jan. Van. Leveringh, a member of the Levering family who returned to Europe. *Cf.* " German Pietists," p. 338.

[5] Johann Gottfried Selig, one of the leaders of the Kelpius Community. For biographical sketch *cf.* " German Pietists."

[6] Stephen Mumford (born 1639; died July, 1701) is accredited with being the founder of the Seventh-day Baptist Church in America. *Cf.* " German Pietists," pp. 136 et seq. Also " Seventh Day Baptists in Europe and America," by Professor Corlies F. Randolph, Vol. II, Plainfield, N. J.

[7] Rev. Tobias Eric Biorck, pastor of the Swedish Lutheran Church at Christiana (Wilmington, Del.).

[8] Maria Elizabeth Gerber in Virginia. The identity of this person has not been solved.

There are no records known that any Germans were in Virginia at that early day, yet some of the early records in the Halle orphanage seem to indicate their presence.

[9] Magister Johannes Fabricius, professor in the University of Altdorf, tutor of Johannes Kelpius.

These letters, as will be seen, are somewhat rhapsodical, and filled with obscure illusions to mystical subjects and scriptural quotations. A vein of true piety, however, pervades every missive, the whole being an evidence of the survival of superstition at that late day, strangely mingled with the observed facts of science.

---

[10] Hester Palmer in Flushing, Long Island. Identity not established. Evidently a member of Steven Mumford's congregation.

BOOKPLATE OF THE LONDON SOCIETY FOR PROPAGATING THE GOSPEL IN
FOREIGN PARTS.

REMAINS OF THE ANCHORITE CELL OF MAGISTER KELPIUS.

NEGATIVE BY JULIUS F. SACHSE, LIT. D., 1895.

I.

LETTER TO HEINRICH JOHANN DEICHMAN, LONDON, ENGLAND.

COPY OF A LETTER FROM PENNSYLVANIA TO LONDON, TO MR. HEINRICH JOHANN DEICHMAN.

February 24th, 1697.

Faithful Fellow Champion Deichman!

YOUR esteemed favor received with joy, and there resounds from "The Call to Wisdom," which you enclosed, such an echo in our spirit, as though wisdom herself had meant us. We behold the harmony of divine discipline by virtue of a sympathetic agreement of your centre with ours, and although the radiant roads from and to the latter, cross each other in an endless manner, yet with all this diversity, the aspect of the upper huts of our mother, manifold wisdom, becomes more dear and joyous. Therefore we are not angry because of your cross and opposition roads, just as you, we hope, are not angry with ours, because, indeed, from the stroke of the cross, the bright colors of the sign of peace must be born, just as Solomon from David. The radii of our cross are directed at present from the centre exteriorly, when, however, the Lord is willing to unite these outward-turned extremities of our cross in their central point, He alone knows, and to Him alone this is possible. Hence it is not my intention to pen with ink of our color, the letters Y. L. (Your Love), because your love is sealed in its place. We only long for the revelation in and from out the heart of the love of God, and the more anxiously we bear, the more carefully the Lord hides us from the dragon, that watches so carefully for the birth, in order to devour it.

Fight thou with us, thou faithful soul, and lead all thy relatives forth into the same battle, and suffer no strange trumpet of a prince operating through fame in the air, to separate our united phalanx under the banner of the Lion and the Lamb. (we must long for in hopeful patience, as later on, the Father at times, renders the waiting sweet).

The Lord once said: We love him rightly, for whom we can wait a long time; he, whom we love but little, from him we soon depart. The Lord hath also waited long for us, ere we received this desire, in which blissful, hoping waiting, I remain with cordial embrace in the love of Jesus

thine eternally united
J. KELPIUS.

P. S. Most worthy brother, the longer I write, the more ardent my spirit becometh in the desire for the revelation of our hope, because all pens or quills, or even bodily cohabitation, though these modify the longing somewhat, do but little or naught for the cause. How often am I in the spirit more exactly round about you, than I am with those with whom I corporeally dwell in Kedar. Therefore I kiss the Father's hand that hath led me into this desert as into a chamber. For verily! had I remained in London with Mecken and Clerk, we should have done harm never to be told unto each other, as I now clearly see, as we love each other cordially, and they were loth to let me go, hoping in spirit to continue the work vigorously. I went with joy into this desert, as into a garden of roses, and I knew not at that time, that it was the furnace of affliction in which the Lord was about to purify and to prove me, and now I see it, since the heat hath somewhat passed by, and I praise the Father, our Lord Jesus Christ, that He willed such good unto me. But enough hereof! My best regards to Mecken & Clerk, if they still survive, as I hope, and grow with us in the same hope; it is but for a little while, as I hope, and we shall speak unto each other differently, far differently than heretofore, and then shall no man take our joy from us, for the faithful and true witness will not suffer us to be constantly in unrest.

I am in no wise displeased with them, that they were offended in us and, in a measure, delivered us unto death. We have, indeed, often been brought near to the gates of death, and the coldness of death, which David dreaded so much, is not yet past. Now where our loss has been their salvation (as above indicated) how much more will our life be their assumption (proslepsis), when the Lord shall awaken us from the dead. We certainly had had sufficient cause, to be offended in them; if, however, this being were to continue in growth, where would the accretion be, and the love that is founded upon forgiveness from the heart, and forgiveness upon the knowledge of one's own faults, and this knowledge is founded upon that great humility which we all lacked in spite of our great knowledge. But the Lord knoweth how to humble the proud, and how to bend that which in us is rigid by means of His fatherly cross-blows with which our ways are interwoven. To Him be praise, honor, power and glory for ever, world without end. Amen.

AN ANCIENT HOROSCOPE CAST BY THE MYSTICS ON THE WISSAHICKON.

II.

LETTER TO HEINRICH JOHANN DEICHMAN, LONDON, ENGLAND.

To the Same, May 12th, 1699, through Jan von Lewenigh (Delivered).

Faithful brother and fellow of the tribulation, of which, at this time, all partake that hope in patient and longing waiting for the glorious appearance of our Lord and Saviour Jesus Christ.

J HEAR with special joy, how you show in your last letter, happily delivered together with a package by Mr. Schaeffer, your heart unto us as in a mirror, and how you permit us to see in what manner you are being purified in the furnace of the covenant, even so, that you feel, that your experience was not the lot of the children of God for many centuries. Just as I have made mention in my first letter to you, of similar experiences of ours, but especially of mine own, concerning such as the Lord from the beginning to this hour uniteth more firmly; but, afterwards, for upwards of a whole year, my experience is such, that the water hath not only often encompassed my soul, as you say of yourself, but I have even sunk in the deepest and bottomless slough of despond. So you, too, at the beginning of that state, did compose a lay of woe, sent to me through Falkner, so that I must conclude, that the entire body of Christ is now suffering on earth, nor do I understand this to be an ordinary suffering, but rather such as extendeth from Gethsemane to Golgotha; yea, what shall I say, it hath not yet come to the . . . branch! The worst, the thrust of death, is still behind, when I shall atone before no common one . . . on the cross, or Jebusite, as Herod, or mystic imagination and dreams (but I am not speaking) (will reveal the right mystic way, which the world did hide) but of a real, where, essentially, this is done once and for all time, and from out of which a necessary transmutation as to body, soul and spirit resulteth. I have, indeed, heard and read much of many that have died, risen, ascended, yea, descended with a virgin body, and now filling therewith their former body in such a manner, that the new covereth the old, as hides or pelts cover the hut of Moses, etc., the worthiness of which I do not impeach; yet sad experience hath hitherto taught, that most men, after such advance, have not only not outstripped the others, but some have been made subservient to others, and have, in part, become unlike themselves in a deterior altitude. The words of Partus (Plato ?) are clear indeed, on which my faith is founded, that none in this life is preferred before another, much less, that one shall be the cause efficient of another's resurrection. Great speculations on this subject are of no avail, much less availeth imagination, which latter, with those who had some true relations, was at last regarded as such, or at least blended therewith, though they consider themselves free from all mixture, for they do it, though eventual acts may approve of speculation, and it has been tried, bringing on many a great fall, of which I could adduce sufficiently many examples, and indeed of such who in their palmy days would not have yielded to any one in England on account of their inspiration; but the same are such as by these events are compelled to hide themselves in their chambers, until the wrath be completely past, before which they were unwilling, at that time, to stoop, thinking themselves, as being perfectly cleansed and purified, sufficiently strong, until that wrath be cast upon the ground. And although such a fall, however great it is (see Psalm 62, 2 Gen.) might not eternally cast them down, that is, according to their inner spark of faith; as long as we, that is, the simple and quiet, step most securely. He that believeth, hasteneth not. He that hath said, He would come, will come assuredly, and without our running before; the wise virgins will be awakened, all at the same time, and they go forth and enter, all at the same time, into the joy of their Lord, none of them runneth before or precedeth another, and, therefore, we should not regard the so called preference in the kingdom of God, because herein there existeth no precedence and order, or emulation, as is the case in academies and at courts of the world, but the greatest is as the least, and Christ sayeth: " The first shall be last, and the last shall be first." But if any one is of the opinion (I still call it an opinion) although he that thinketh so, regardeth it as his own opinion, that is, he or she, or he and she at the same time, the masculine birth for the universal redemption of groaning creation, as well as those that have received the firstlings of the Spirit, become God-bearing.

Now then, in the name of the Lord, let them step forth and finish this work so long desired, to my bliss and joy, as well as to that of all creation, and then we may call it in another opinion.

But, worthy brother, forgive me, if I continue as an unbelieving Thomas to present to your mind the example of our dearest Saviour Jesus and his precursor John, not to speak of others, as I only represent a biga (two-horse-chariot) of eternal grace, because, at present and heretofore, men have always been speaking of Z.[2] However much these kept themselves hidden before their assumption of office, however silent they were concerning their future, but they kept themselves in all things in a virgin silence (whereof in the Old Testament, the virgins always remain at home, and a going out in disguise representeth something properly) until that hour which was destined for them in the calendar of eternity, and then she stepped forth not with pen and ink, but in strength and might, which no foe could withstand, there you see how very much such a biga of eternal grace, even for our times and longer yet (availeth?), but this excessive boasting hereof in the streets of Babylon is somewhat suspicious to me. The cry: " See here! " " See there! " not to speak of the idle personal applications. In a word, the affair will come to pass quite differently than one or several men, yea, even Jesus Christ himself imagines, and though we have revelation

---

[2] Z = possibly an astrological character.

hereof, this revelation oftentimes cannot comprehend the spirit of the instrument, and often falls upon a false application of its person, and, if this will not do, it must be called a figure; now, inasmuch as many have practiced carnal lust in faith, or, at least, have brought about a spiritual mixture. How often, for pity's sake, have these things happened, and still happen even in such through whom it was hoped, salvation should burst forth; and we may perhaps not be so much mistaken in the application, as were the two disciples that journeyed to Emmaus, though we cannot demonstrate it to them, for those unto whom we can re-monstrate it, so that they may know it themselves even without remonstrations, these also stand in just as great danger as the others, in whom it appeared spiritually before God, but did not come to a bursting forth. As then the mystery of the holy gospel (when children that tie a string about a bird's foot and permit it to fly upward, and the bird thinking its freedom attained, but the children may pull it down to them at will) is fulfilled, wherein the spirit of evil permits them to soar on high in knowledges and visions, caring little about their freedom of ascension, if only he can make them descend at will by means of the rope fastened to their feet and incorporated with their earthly dwelling.

Dearest brother! Unto your opened wound, oil may be perhaps more agreeable than salt and pungent wine? which oil you would fain choose and expect of me, as, doubtless, you are bruised and dejected in mind sufficiently, and, believe me, that I am loth to swim in this element, as I would rather enjoy and gently glide with my beloved on evening clouds, but I am loth to storm with the north wind through the garden of God! But, my faithful heart, when I consider the dangerous place where you are and in spirit see, how some by bland gifts . . . seek to gouge out your eye and to bind your hands, after having shorn you of your locks of liberty, I would rather see you with Samson turning the mill-stone of exterior hard work (as we have done and at times still do, rather than see you basking in the lap of your beloved spiritual Delilah.)

I dearly love F. L. and his associates, and their writings have often strengthened me and raised me up, but I wish from my heart, we may not see this sad drama more. So I also know, how those dear souls Quedlinburg (whom I spiritually embrace and kiss) founded upon the corner-stone of our salvation, have been so powerfully edified, after having laid aside so many rudiments, and I hope, they will also discard the remaining superfluities, and hasten to the purpose; therefore, I deem myself too paltry and miserable to teach them anything, because I am so fain to see, that, being rid of all teachers and martinets, we might be taught, enlightened and inspired and directly united with the head, the only high priest of our salvation, which, of course, cannot and will not be accomplished without previous dearth, discipline, temptation, cross (or whatever we may call it, as previously indicated by me), nor without the final lunge of death, although thereafter nothing shall take us captive and detain us; hence, we cannot but expect the bursting forth of salvation from Jesus Christ, in, from and through us all, because we all are but one body, and He, Jesus of Nazareth, remaineth the glorified theanthrope, from whom the life of the Father welleth and bursteth forth. Behold, dear brother, this manifest and through His apostles manifested truth is not unknown to you; inasmuch, however, as we see so many and various pseudo-saviours in the theatre of these our revolutions, it were not strange, if our countenances were somewhat turned away from the only true one, and if we looked infatuated upon another guest-brother's beauty, yea, angelic and cherub-like clearness, and thus forsook our truest and most beautiful bridegroom amongst all, and if we became faithless or even adulterous and would thus contaminate our virgin garment or even lose it; we recognize, indeed, among all these forms, the proximity of salvation, but so, that we may not embrace some folly because of too great ardour and heat of desire, as some men and women in their too ardent and passionate devotions have done, soaring perhaps too high, and then being humiliated, they took heed, as then the danger is truly and ineffably great, but not so great, as when we in spirit desert our most true and loving Jesus for the sake of others (though they were angels), and become mixed with them, as indicated before, and you stand before this matter in greater danger on account of various circumstances (as we, for the sake of necessary assistance, sometimes do that which we otherwise do not approve of, as we here).

But as our dear Mr. Schirmer, in Halle, is reported to have said to Mr. Schaeffer: 'He would probably, find the devil in Pennsylvania,' so we are not ignorant of that which he is thinking of, but as Mr. Lange (of Hungary, if I err not) said to Falkner & Koester: 'Ye will also find the dear Lord Jesus in Pennsylvania'; hence He standeth at our right hand as a hero and screeneth us from all fiery onslaughts of Satan, and because His pure wisdom hath upon her tongue both the sharp law and the gentle grace, Prov. 3. 16, so we also are strengthened and comforted in all things and through all things, as we have experienced in ourselves and in others, where we, from a distance, impartially observe the deeds or the stumblings of every one of your round-table-companies.

But enough hereof! If now, dear brother, you find some assuredness in your heart, to come to us, do not think, that my dear Sohlige by his walking about, is aiming at you or your congress, as I am certain, you will be drawn by quite a different principle in coming hither, as our dear Schaefer, or others were, who from hence ran back again, hoping to teach the world or even the saints. For, how you will fare here, we already see in spirit, and I have been thinking of this before, hoping the salt would be more agreeable to you, than if I had placed before you mere peace. Compare the signs of the times with each other (whereof you have made mention in your letter) and you will easily, with Amos, be able to make a resolution to hide yourself, which you, according to our opinion can do no longer, inasmuch as matters have progressed too far, and your faith hardly reaches so far, that you would believe, it would rain manna into your tent (though I cannot find any thing in your letter to justify your giving up your present engagement entirely).

We cordially received Schaefer and gave him the choice among

3

7 or 5 different places, among our acquaintances and friends,
where he might have enjoyed his bread in quietude; if he had only
tutored the child of the house, he might have, after so many
wanderings and ups and downs, been able to come to rest and
permit God to prepare his soul and fix his purpose. But his heart
always drew him to his nation: Swedes, Finlanders and Indians,
which 3 resemble each other very much, in order to do good among
them, as he thinks; and he went amongst them, and we parted
from each other in love, as we left the door open for him, to come
back to us, if he should not find among his nation that which he
thought he would. But when at last, his soul shall be brought
to rest, the Lord alone knows, for he himself is without method
to attain this end, on the contrary, he is desirous of converting
and strengthening others, though he himself confesses he has no
grounds, and thus many impede their own progress in various
manners, and cannot enter into their rest because of mere un-
belief, standing so firmly upon themselves. Now, who could think,
that our human way could be a wrong way, in so much as to be
unwilling to turn therefrom. God be merciful unto such and unto
us all!

Now, whatever you do, do it in faith, that the Lord will provide, and doubt thou not. Neither be thou afeard of the lions,
nor of the bears, nor of serpents, nor any animal, but step upon
their necks in the power of God, believing that they can harm no
one but him that is afeard of them. Now, if you find the means
to come hither, do not wait for Fox, but come in thy strength
and faith which the Lord will give you, lest Alva, that is, the talk
of an infidel move you and untoward thoughts seduce you. I seek
not to persuade you, and for all the world I would not have your
faith founded on me, nor on anyone else, but upon God alone.
Do not make too much of this enterprise, as though you would
hereby evade Babylon and all temptations, nor yet too little, as
though this place were not more comfortable for your circumstances, to hide you in your exile, than London is and safety lies
in a middle course, that is, in child-like simplicity. If this comes
to pass, we shall, no doubt, receive more ample information con-

cerning many things, than we have received hitherto, especially concerning Catharina B. v. B., whereof we knew not a word, and how greatly we mourn this, is ineffable, so much so, that our heart would break; I would rather have imagined, the sun would be illumined by the moon, than that this would-be (as Maxan called him after his death, in consequence of which, he was imprisoned for a whole year and robbed of the presence of God, because he intrusted this one with several secrets, and as he related to Hattenbach, as is known) and black magician could darken and blacken this luminous sun (i. e. Catharina). And he may prefer cutting a figure, inasmuch as his second marriage, or whoredom, is sufficient proof and shows what he was hankering after, namely, lust of the flesh, which he could not satisfy in this pious soul, and what Seelig writes hereof, will, no doubt, become true. But she may be a figure before the judgment of God, how they began at the house of God, and how God in her, being the purest and best soul I have ever known, how they did begin to lay low in the dust all that which is sublime in the eyes of men. And it may possibly be, that she, on account of her rare gifts and special virtues (as then Jesus Christ, himself but a child, did distinguish her, though in outward splendor and knowledge of many things she had advanced considerably, whereof no one should boast, but rather fear). She was idolized by many and may have delighted therein, wherefore the Lord did abash her and caused her to be clothed in sack-cloth or goat skin, that she might forget her excessive wanderings, and hide herself from the knowledge of men. Then many a great saint will in secret rejoice, thinking himself to become great through her fall, and to make himself esteemed by judging and condemning her, just as he seeth and toucheth her exterior, rough sack in which the Lord hideth her, so he manifesteth hereby his internal, thorny and black nature which erstwhile had remained hidden under a radiant sheep skin. Who knows how shortly others may be abashed, who think not only to be standing alone, but also to become foundation-pillars to support the entire superstructure, yea to be such pillars already.

O blessed lowliness! How many fickle spirits flit above thee, whilst Jesus was so lowly and, in all things, like unto His brethren, yea, even more lowly than they; and I should like to know, how Dr. Schmidberg and others welcomed her, when she returned. The poor child, no doubt must have been compelled to run the gauntlet and to sing from the Song of Songs: Look not upon me because I am black, because the sun hath looked upon me: my mother's children were angry with me; they made me the keeper of the vineyards; but mine own vineyard have I not kept. It may have been a special providence, that I did not receive her letter at that time, for all things must arrive at their appointed time. Still, I should like to know what therein was. But if it had for its author . . . , I can easily imagine what it contained. Write thou to her, prithee, with my cordial greetings, and though I should like to chat with her for an hour, to bring to her heart several things, what the Lord hath done by us both, yet I would not allure her forth from her rest and quietude. I doubt not but the Lord will bless her in time, in that He hath through her blessed so many; and because she, too, is as His sheep in His hand, so neither that . . . nor any other man will be able to snatch her from out His hand. Amen.

What we as brethren have written, you may communicate at the same time (because the one explaineth the other) without fear and reserve. For although I have touched upon several particulars and have written rather frankly (but Seelig has remained in general topics) I have no doubt but that all honest and upright disciples in Christ according to His doctrine, will readily assimilate the salt, though it disgusteth those who wantonly would remain effeminate weaklings. But do not omit corresponding very frequently with us, because herein I perceive the special hand of God, therefore I have also procured for you a good address, as you may see from what I have enclosed, the which you are to hand to W. S. Send us the acts with diligence, in that our friends crave for them and, if possible, something of Portage, who is entirely unknown to us. We had written about one or two pages; now if these be addressed to H. B. in care of this merchant W. S., they will reach their destiny in security.

Now, if ever you come to us, all things shall be made good. Please to give my kindest regards to Mecken and inform him of the fact, that I am not at all afeard of his letter, inasmuch as I have become so hardened in this desert, that I can possibly endure corporeal punishment, though undeserved. May the Lord alone strengthen us through an extraordinary power (for such is ours in these days) that we may reward the word of His patience, until that He come. Yes, come, Lord Jesus. Amen. Hallelujah.

Yours, J. K.

SYMBOL OF THE MYSTICAL EPHRATA COMMUNITY ON THE COCALICO, LANCASTER COUNTY, PENNA.

III.

LETTER FROM JOHANN SELIG
TO H. J. DEICHMAN, LONDON, ENGLAND.

COPY OF THE LETTER WHICH JOHANN SEELIG TO THE SAME
WITH THIS DID SEND.

Dearly beloved Brother in the Lord:—

YOUR letter has partly comforted, partly grieved, and yet again encouraged us, in that the Lord in one and the same spirit (unto as many of us as stand in one spirit of the pure knowledge of His wondrous judgments) hath given us to perceive, whither such apparent calamities at this time are aimed and directed, the which is lost sight of by magicians, but is brought home unto them assuredly in divine power from the simple ground of faithmagic, to the consternation of the whole world, for whereby that adept in the black art though he could soar aloft and crush his opponent, even thereby he may be brought down, whilst his opponent riseth in divine power. Behold, how the principal person is already acting in the final destruction of the world through his false—morning star or harbinger! Through this their confusion, there is instituted from the simple and childlike ground of faith, the true lovefeast or supper of the marriage of the Lamb (thus Apocalypse 19 should have been rendered in our German Bible). As no mention is made of this supper by the church and the reformation Baals up to this time, as a witness against them, that they do not belong to the blessed that are called thereunto, until after holding such a lovefeast, the King himself in person appeareth, and the afore-mentioned person who will then also appear, and bear in his flesh the centre of the magic ground of the dark world, bringing it to a close.

My dear little brother, we, indeed, had many things to speak of and to write of, but how is it possible, that the above imperishable soul-spark wedded unto the light of its sophic bride, should be able to manifest itself properly through these awkward, unproportioned organs of our present miserable body, wherein the same lies captive besides? Nothing is pleasing to the sight of this spark, not even the most beautiful colors of our aurora, because such are not the fixed body, though veritable signs of the same. Therefore, we especially labor and cry with our beloved to God our Father, Psalm 63: O God, thou art my God; early will I seek thee: my soul thirsteth for thee, my flesh longeth for thee in a dry and thirsty land, where no water is. And how often doth my flesh yearn thus! The flesh of Christ in us longeth to come out of the pathless desert and dry flesh of this body to the upper hut of the body that is not fashioned with hands from the waters above. Yet the beloved desireth, in no other manner than through divine birth-right, to sit in the spoiled lap of his bride, passing from such dryness and pathless desert and saying, that I may be seen thus in thy holy doing.

Therefore, let us be unanimous, nor let us tear off the swaddling-clothes of the discipline of our Father, as naughty children do, that afterward were bound with ropes; but nowadays many children are neither swathed nor bound, therefore filling the vessel too heavily, and, in turn, it is meted out unto them heavily. O blessed bond wherewith Paul was bound, when he writeth of himself: " I in spirit bound! " considering that some are unwilling to see the mystery of this binding in spirit, or unwilling to resign themselves thereunto. Hence there ariseth: 1. a restless running about from place to place without use and fruit of edification, either of one's self or of another; 2. a life according to one's own advice, caring little for that which one's neighbor giveth in love and faith, but . . . Of God and His Spirit; 3. all manner of fickle imagination concerning one's self and one's deeds to which we were called in the world or in the church, as one imagines; 4. spiritual luxuriance or lewdness according to the word of the prophet, Old Testament, consisting in a constant desire of devotion in our own circle and also in behalf of others, breaking thereby the faith-link of Peter, namely: abstinence 2 Feb. 45. 6, especially at this time, when the impure, astral Venus desires to run constantly parallel to and act equally with our true philadelphian spirits of love, which are the essential body of heavenly wisdom, against which there is no better remedy than the drawing rope and that which the Lord, through the raisin, so truly testifieth at the last: Put on a rough coat and hide thyself, so that no one may know thee. That which is written in confirmation of this, Ep. 34 and Psalm XLXX, is of importance; 5. there ariseth a foolish nuisance, in that we cannot accommodate ourselves to the varying forms of Saul, where the Lord put on his cloth in distinct manners, but we think an impure spirit is making his abode therein. Now, as that one doth not fly into a passion, but understandeth well, why the Lord hath, for a time, hidden them, not only from men, but also from one another. (Yea, also from one's self in kind, as David prayeth therefor, 2. Sam. 22. LXX. Lord redeem or save from myself: (these words, I have added) ; 6. such unbridled liberty easily leadeth into a barren . . . temptation; as such an one often thinketh himself in the midst of hell, and almost immediately thereafter he declares he is in heaven, by which declaration, the ignorant are dazzled, as being beyond the true bounds of the process of Christ (in which something may come to pass which has a similarity, just as the astral Venus with the sophistic, which is but an astral motion, whereby the sensate elementary part, which lies below, just as the earth beneath the stars, is thus affected). In this connection men have indulged in another folly arising in them from ignorance, in that they constantly look at the accidents that may strike their exterior part, and are blind to the danger therein, especially at this time, soul . . . may. For then they consider themselves well secured and to have done almost everything, if they are exact in matters of external clothing, eating and drinking, in business and in their form of outward devotion, and hence they enjoy quietude, but they are unwilling to comprehend aught of the firmament of the astral principle, where the need is greatest, nor will they suffer being told that such disturbs their devotion; 7. there finally ariseth the great evil, namely, the aforementioned abode of Satan, wherein we are confirmed in error and work disgrace upon disgrace. May our faithful God and Father of our Saviour grant that none of His be brought so low, but may He deliver them from the tribulation in the 7th, that they may not be united with the evil one.

My dear little brother, pardon my prolixity, I am not seeking to instruct thee, perhaps thou'rt more learned and stronger than I am. I am only trying to roll a part of my burden upon thy shoulders, hoping thou wilt help me bear it. What shall I say, when I think of the merciful, dear heart of God our Father who hath, for these many years in this desert, preserved several of us, especially me and dear brother Kelpius, from the arrows of destruction. What shall I say, when I think of the powerful eagle wings, upon which His providence hath lifted us poor worms, and borne us and conducted us wonderfully. My heart is melting away in tears and will not suffer me to pursue the thought, nor can this be, for it still lieth in mysterious wisdom, as a child in the womb hidden, and, in season due, its joy shall be made manifest.

My bodily health is rather poor; do not be too obscure in your letter, but open your heart unto us, as well as you may and just as the Lord permitteth, especially in regard to C. Reecken and others.

The religions here are in constant opposition, nor is this at all surprising, for they are *the* Jordan, of whose roaring waves and cataracts David in his exile in the desert, Psalm 42, singeth, which will endure until that Joshua and Elijah come and divide the river which is rightly called Jordan, that is, a division and ejection of judgment into victory, whence another Jordan will arise, that is, the doctrine of the judgment, which will flow in loveliness, for in the significance, as a figure of the cross of wisdom, is contained in the near Jordan. Greetings, etc., etc.

P. S. to my letter. On perusing this letter, I was amazed at myself, regarding with wonderment: 1. the long, 2. the prickly, 3.

the rough sack in which I was clad while writing, having resolved to write something totally different, but my spirit was broken, and my heart directed elsewhither, and my mind was led in bonds, whither it would not; I was fain to retain the letter, were I not as yet bound. I, therefore, resign the matter wholly to the merciful Father of our Saviour Jesus Christ, who knoweth why this had to be thus, though I, for the most part, know not, yet recognize this fact, especially as to persons, thinking of so many personalities.

My heart would fain melt away in tears of blood, both when I consider the tribulations to come, and also for gratitude and joy, when I think of the salvation, how His fatherly hand hath already saved us from so many snares of the hunter, and poured His blessings upon us. This again awakens the slumbering hopes, so that I commend all things unto the Lord with a believing heart, for He will do all things well.

Farewell.

SEAL OF THE SISTERHOOD OF SARON ON THE COCALICO (FROM ANCIENT EPHRATA DOCUMENT).

IV.

LETTER TO STEVEN MOMFORT IN RHODE ISLAND.

To Mr. Steven Momfort in Long Island[1] in America.

1699, 11. December.

Dear Friend and Brother:

IN fellow-fighting in that Free and Royal Spirit which strives for the Prize of the first Resurrection when in this Midnight the Cry of the Bridegroom's coming is sounded forth among the Virgin waiters for the Preparation of the Temple Body, wherein the King of Glory and Father of the coming Eternity is to enter. Your great desire for to be a little further informed of the Principles and Practizes of those People that go under the Name of Pietists, what they hold as Doctrin differing from others, what their Discipline is and what Methods they use in their own Country; this desire I will hope, doth not arise from the Root of that Athenian Curiosity to hear some new thing; But rather you being one among thousands in Juda, who sees how since that glorious Primitive Church of Christ Jesus the Apostacy hath run in a continual current till this very day, and though this Stream hath divided itself in many smaller Rivulets, under several Names of more reformed Purity, yet you are not ignorant how they derive their Emanation from one Spring and tend to the same end, Viz. that the Woman in the Wilderness might be carried away by the Flood. Therefore you, as a Remnant of her seed, long for to see your Mother and groan for the Manifestation of her children. No wonder then, if your continual Gazing upon this Supercaelestial Orb and Sphier from whence with her

---

[1] Should be Rhode Island.

47

Children, causeth you to observe every new Phoenomena, Meteors, Stars and various Colours of the Skei, if peradventure you may behold at last an Harbinger as an Evidence of that great Jubelee or Restitation of all things and glorious Sabbathismos or the continual days of Rest without intervening or succeeding Nights, whereof God hath spoken by the mouth of all his Prophets since the world began (Acts 3, 21) and whereof both the Testaments prophesie in every Title and Iota. If now this late Revolution in Europe (not to speak of that in other parts) which in the Roman Church goes under the Name of Quietism, in the Protestant Church under the Name of Pietism, Chiliasm, and Philadelphianism, If I say this together or one in Special purtends any thing to this effect. I do not question, but it will be your as well as my desire, who would rejoyce not only to give you full satisfaction as to this, but to see with you, yet in our days, that happy day, which when its new Earth swallows all that forementioned Floud and where its glorious Sun causeth all other Stars and Phoenomena to disappear, no Night succeeds it, but that the Night is swallowed up in ye Day, Darkness into Light, Death into Life, Judgment into Victory, Justice into Mercy, all imperfect Metals into Gold, and Gold itself is refined seven times, and all Churches and Virgins comprised into the one Dove (Cant. 6, 9), then all the Sons of God will shout for joy as they did in the Beginning, when God was all in all, as he will be all in all, when again the End hath found its Beginning. Amen! Halleluiah!

Dear and worthy friend, though unknown to the Flesh but known in that better, yea in the best Line and highest descent in the Life of our Immanuel, whose day we rejoyce to hear of and more to see, as well within us as without us, in its Depth, Hight, Breadth and Length, through the whole palsed and groaning Creation, as well as in our Mother Jerusalem above and Beneath! How can I write the particulars of the Quietists, Chiliasts or Philadelphians, whose Fame is spread in all the 4 quarters of the now Christianity. They first sprang in Italy, in Rome itself (and are increased now through the whole Roman Church in many

Millions, though they was and are still depressed) 15 or 20 years before the Pietists or Chiliasts in Germany and Switzerland (where the first Reformation) in the year '89 and '90, with a swift increase through the whole Nation, so that their Branches also did break forth into other Nations, as in England under the name of Philadelphians. This Penn is too dull to express the extraordinary Power the Pietists and Chiliasts among the Protestants in Germany (and especially in Saxony) and Switzerland was endued with in their Infancy. This only I say, as one who hath read the Histories, that since the days of the Apostels, such Miraculous Powers and operations have not been manifested as in a matter of 3½ years among these. And like as the Miracles wrought by God through the Hand of Moyses was for the main part in the outward Creation or Macrocosm, the Miracles of Jesus the Messia on the Bodys of Man or Microcosm, so these in our days was wrought (much like unto them in the days of the Apostles) on the Soul and more interiour parts by Ectases, Revelations, Inspirations, Illuminations, Inspeakings, Prophesies, Apparitions, Changings of Minds, Transfigurations, Translations of their Bodys, wonderful Fastings for 11, 14, 27, 37 days, Paradysical Representations by Voices, Melodies, and Sensations to the very perceptibility of the Spectators who was about such persons, whose condition as to the inward condition of their Souls, as well as their outward Transactions, yea their very thoughts they could tell during the time of their Exstacies, though they had never seen nor heard of the Persons before.

These and many other Gifts continued as is said, for a matter of three years and a half among all sorts of Persons, Noble, and ignoble, Learned and unlearned, Male and female, young and old, very conspiciously and generally Protestants chiefly, and some Papists, and with some though more refined such and like Gifts last till this very day.

Thus partly I have declared how they was baptized with such energical drops out of that supercaelestial Pillar of Cloud by Gifts and miraculous Manifestations of the Powers from on high.

Now will I tell in short in what a craggy, uneven yea dark

wilderness they have been led since, when hitherto they have been
baptized with the fiery Pillar of many inward and outward Tribulations, Sorrows, Temptations, Refinings, Purifications (but nevertheless this Fiere casts such a Light befor'm that securs'm from
the persuing Might and dark influence of Egypt and guides'm in
that beloved land and City.) This must be through many Tribulations as the Apostels have witnessed, so they felt it and feel it still
very smartly. For when these things begun to ferment every where,
1. The Students in the Universities forsake their former way of
Learning and applied themselves wholly to Piety and Godliness,
(from whence their name was derived) leaving and some burning
their heathenish Logiks, Rhetoriks, Metaphysiks. 2. The Laymen
or Auditors begun to find fault with the Sermons and Lifes of
their Ministers, seeing there was nothing of Ye Power of the Holy
Ghost, nor of the Life of Christ and his Apostels. 3. The children
under the Information and Tuition of Pietists, (for the Students
applied themselves chiefly to the Education of Children, as they
do till this day with great, yea extraordinary success) begun to
reproof their Parents if they was working an Lye or unrighteous-
ness! yea some in their tender years came to witness strange things
of the Invisible worlds. Till at last Demetrius with his Craftsmen
begun to see and hear that not only in Lipzig, (from which University this Motion first begun to spread abroad) but almost
throughout all Germany and adjacent Contrys these Pietists did
persuade and turn away much People, saying that the Form of
Godliness without the Power thereof is meer Idolatry and superstition; Yea they saw, how that not only this their craft was endangered by these and set at nought, but also the Temple or Universities of the great Goddess Dianoria or Reason and Ratiocina-
tion (which is quite different from that Dionoria or Understanding or Unction whereof John witnesses i Joh. 5. 19. c. 2, 27.)
should be despised and her Magnificence (thus the Rectors in the
Universities are titled) should be destroyed, if in the place of
Dianoria, the Sophia from on high should be adored and instead of

Temples or Universities, the Hearts of men should be consecrated. (Excuse me, dear Heart, that I thus run into an Allegoricall Application, for the very same Comedy was played as you read in the Acts of the Apostels, only the time and persons changed.) Thus the Battel and Insurrection begun, which lasteth till this day.

The Anti-Pietists (so their Adversaries are pleased to call themselves) betook themselves to the secular Arm. But several Princes being partly inclined to the Principles of the Pietists, partly convinced of a superior Agent in these things, took them in their Protection, especially the Elector of Brandeb. In the Principality of Brunswick and Lunebourg, the course was otherwise, for in the very beginning 3 Bishops or Supirts was removed their offices; the same happened in other Countries and Cities, as Erford, Lipzik, Quedlinbourg, Halberstad, Hambourg, Hassen Cassel, where and in Switzerland lately several Ministers are removed and some banished the Country. Thus they increased under the Cross. As for any peculiar Badge or Mark, they have none being above these trifling affections) or any peculiar Church Ceremony or Discipline which should cause a Shism or branch a new sect. For they are not ignorant of the wilderness wherein the Church is and hath been hitherto, and in what a glory she will appear when she comes up from the Wilderness leaning on her beloved. Cant. 8. 5. They see well enough how all the Reformations and Revolutions in this last Age as well as theirs are but Apparitions of the fair colours of the Aurora or Break of the day, mixed with many uncleanness wherein there is no stay (as my beloved Brother and faithful Fellow-Pilgrim in this Wilderness state Seelig hath written) for they are not the substance or sun itself though the various beautiful Apparitions of the Skie, should entice one allmost enamoured in them and to mistake the Harbinger for the King! whom to meet they prepare themselves earnestly, some of 'm laying aside all other engagements whatever, trimming their Lamps and adorning themselves with white silky Holiness and golden Righteousness, that they may be found worthy, when the Bridegroom comes, to receive him with confidence and joy and to bring him in the House of their Mother, where He will drink with'm that new spicy wine of the Kingdom in all everlasting Progresses. That we also may prepare ourselves with our whole endeavours continually I wish heartily, who do recommend you in the Clifts of the FoundationRock of our Salvation, Jesus Christ. Remaining your fellow Traveller in this blessed work and best engagement.

JOHANNES KELPIUS.

Dated in the Wilderness.

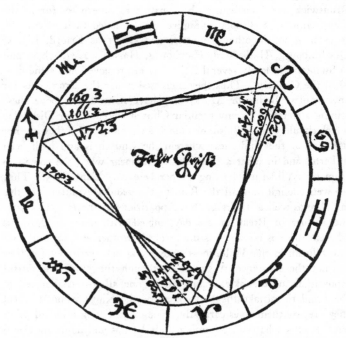

ANCIENT ASTROLOGICAL CHART, AS CAST BY THE EARLY MYSTICS ON THE WISSAHICKON.

ERICUS TOBIAS BIÖRCK.
PASTOR OF THE SWEDISH LUTHERAN CHURCH AT CHRISTIANA (WILMINGTON, DEL.).
PHOTOGRAPH FROM ORIGINAL CANVAS IN SWEDEN.

V.

LETTER TO REV. ERIC BIORCK, CHRISTIANA (WILMINGTON), DELAWARE.

(*Translation*)

To Rev. Magister Eric Biorck,

Pastor at Christianna.

Immanuel.

May Jehovah remember thee, that thou mayest see the good things of his elect; may he remember thee for the sake of his favor toward his people, that thou mayest rejoice in the joy of his nation. May he visit in his salvation, that thou mayest glory in his inheritance. Amen!

Psalm cvi. 45.

Very reverend Sir and Friend, Master and friend in Jesus our Saviour, ever to be regarded by me with fraternal love;

In your beloved letter, written on January 10, and received on January 17, through Mr. Jonas B——, I got a twofold proof of your fraternal love, the epistle and the money. Would to God I were truly such as you have outlined, or such as you have judged me with my most beloved Rudman. By day and by night I attend, indeed, that I may cleanse myself from every blemish both of body and of soul, and I perform my rites in the fear of the Lord, and that I may obtain, by grace alone that which is my pattern by nature, through sincere imitation of him; to wit, the adoption as a son, the redemption of our body (Rom. viii, 23. Compare 1 John iii, 1–2; Phil. iii, 11–15; Gal. iv, 5; Apoc. xix, 8; 2 Tim. iv, 8) How many parasangs as yet I may be distant from the scope (aim) prefixed for myself, becometh known to the fellow-soldiers (Asso-

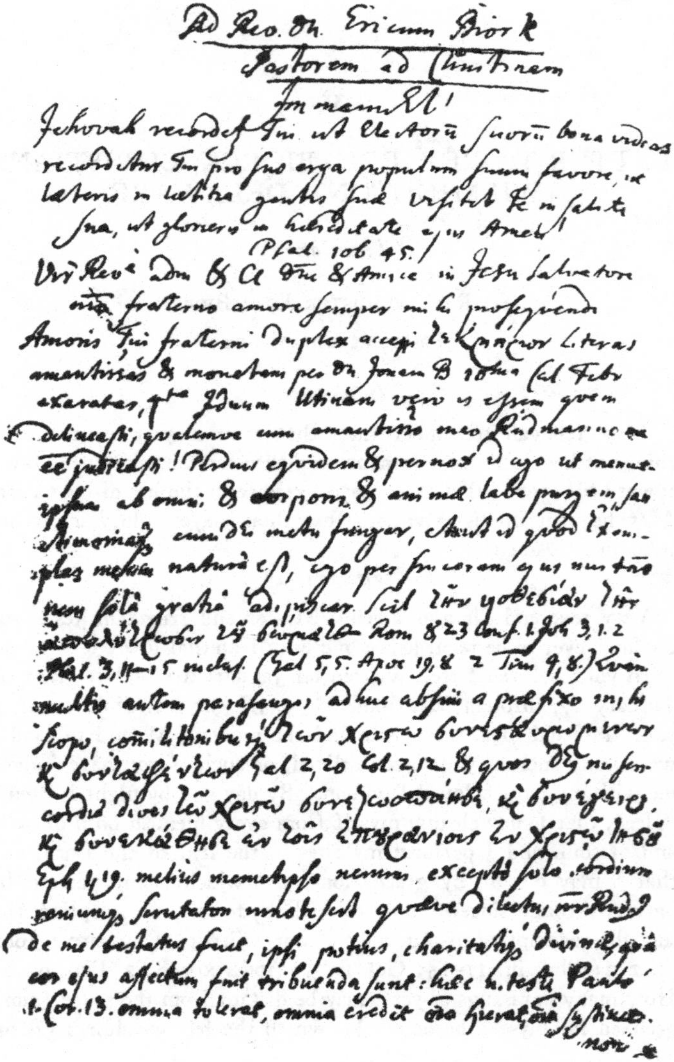

FACSIMILE OF KELPIUS' LETTER TO REV. ERICUS BIORK.

ciates) of those crucified and buried with (in) Christ (Gal. ii, 20,)
and whom God, rich in mercy through Christ, kept secret (in silence) and awakened and placed in the heavenly (places) in Christ
Jesus (Eph. i, 20). Better than myself no one knows (my short-
comings) save alone the searcher of hearts and minds; for that
which our beloved Rudman bore witness concerning me, is to be
attributed rather to himself (Rudman) and to divine charity, where-
withal his heart was affected; these things also, Paul being a witness (1 Cor., xiii). He endureth all, believeth all, hopeth all,
sustaineth all.

naught of evil does he think, nor is he irritable, but he rejoiceth in
verity. Sometimes I am fully convinced, that you, in no wise
spoke for form's sake, as it were, neither your sayings nor your
doings, but that with a sincere heart and with pure affections, as
becomes a true professor of true Christianity, you did unfold the
sentiments of your mind; thus in turn I would you believed that
your mirror reflected the image of him looking therein, i. e. of
yourself; only, had you not enough to do to be conformed to
Christ, our head, in point of a sincere heart and energies (virtues),
never could you notice or admire such in others, though you had
tried it. For who knoweth the business of a man, if not the spirit
of the man, the which is in him: but none among us knoweth the
affairs of God, if not God's spirit. And ye who act in the spirit
of God, the same He acknowledges, and He would have wished
that, also, in others endowed with the same spirit. But the gross,
earthly man, & another divine (theologian) does not understand (grasp) the things which are of the divine spirit, since indeed these be to him folly, and thus (therefore) he cannot know
(understand) those things, inasmuch as (because) they be worthy
of being examined (judged) spiritually. 1 Cor. 2, 14. That is,
amiable man, from whom I have received singular (extraordinary)
joy, that you, namely, although being (notwithstanding your being) busy in the hall according to the manner of your duty
(office), & according to the custom of the Levites, encompassed
round about with animals (sportive?), & scrutinizing, instructing

and sacrificing these into the sanctuary & yet looking into their interior or souls, should finally worship in spirit & in truth. Of which threefold cult of a minister, & of the order of the same, grades, duties, &c. I should have many & knotty points, which I might discourse of, if I should not think it superfluous to begin an enumeration thereof in the presence of a learned man: nor with another end do I allude (treat of) to these, than that our relationship in Christ, & our life in the body, of which you have made mention, may take (assume) a greater increase. Nor is it that, holding fast, he may throw into (infuse) this sacred institution a more righteous (way), & sin surrounding us (Hebr. 12, 1) & the concerns of life (2. Tim. 2, 9), as far as to these things it be expedient, against that we do set watch (a lying out on guard). Verily I confess with you that the necessaries of this life (as they are called) or the things pertaining to life heap up great barriers for (against) the Christian soldier, with the witness Wisdom (chap. IX. 15.) the mortal body weigheth down the spirit & crusheth the understanding, an earthly vessel full of many cares. Nor would you incongruously term these 'strange pursuits,' to wit, we are living on strange (foreign) soil, exiles from Paradise, travellers in this world, nowhere secure, exclaiming with David: Woe is me! who am wandering so long, dwelling with the Cedariani (that I sojourn in Meshech, That I dwell among the tents of Kedar!) i. e. in darkened tents (tabernacles), Psalm 120, 5. The Cedariani, indeed, were the children of Ishmaël, not going to inherit with Isaac, the son of Sarah. From which cause we desire this dark tabernacle of our earthly house to be dissolved, in order that we may obtain an edifice, bright & glorious. But indeed, although Abraham may have interceded for Ishmaël even and may have been heard (granted) by the Lord; we also groan, burthened, unwilling to be freed (unclothed), but clothed over & above, that

---

[1] N. B. The Septuagint in their times read מָזְרִים = mizzorim = strange, with ר (resh = the letter R). In the exemplar (copy) of to-day it is read with ד (daleth = the letter D), Psalm 19, 14. מִזֵּדִים = mizzedim = from the proud.

our mortality may be absorbed in life. 2. Cor. V. 1. Cor. 15, 51.
& N. B. Joh. XI. 26. But of this hidden mystery of the resurrection of the Just, (I will say) not more just now.

But you grieve, most loving little heart, that time must be
expended upon the necessaries of this life? I grieve with you!
But does it seem to you that you have hope in a strait, (does it
seem to you) from this cause that we can perfectly serve God in
this life? There is also to me (hope)! I despair not so much of
the victory (how very distant although as yet I may be (therefrom)) induced (as I am) chiefly by the following arguments
amongst others: I. Paul saith: 1. Cor. 10, 31. Whether ye eat, or
drink, do all to the glory of God, & Col. 3, 17. Whatsoever ye
do both in words & deed, that shall ye do in the name of Jesus,
the Lord, & giving thanks to God the Father through him, compare Eph. 5, 20. 1. Thess. 5, 18. But of the things pertaining
to life they do eat for the most part to eat, to drink, words &
works. All these things can & ought be made subservient to the
glory of God, as saith Paul, therefore the worship of God doth not
present (supply) any hindrance, but an incentive & aid. Whatsoever, he saith, pertaineth to the worship of God unto (by) man,
ought to be perfect. Scarcely was it lawful in the old Testament,
when seeking many things for sacrifices, to make use of an emblem,
because it was not in every way perfect. Hence therefore as if the
field of victory (were) in these very particulars appertaining to life,
it seems to me to be made manifest (open), if in truth (no
wonder) I shall have taken heed thereunto, that (I shall be) free
from the cares of the gentiles, Matt. 6. end, content with my food
& raiment (covering), see Tim. 6, 8, from the desire of becoming
rich & from avarice manifestly averse, ibid., v. 9, 10. (entirely)
not entangled (hampered) by the affairs (concerns, duties) of life,
2. Tim. 2, 4. I say, if not held captive by all these very things,
but I shall have been found master of the same, 1. Cor. 6, 12. Because he is a slave of these things, he cannot serve God, moreover we cannot serve two masters, but in how far he shall have
returned into servitude, & be master over them, in so far does he

render to God a perfect service in these things (hence appear the degrees of perfection) nevertheless dominion consisteth not in possessing nothing (for what sort of king is he without subjects) but in the mind from the things possessed, not in a possessed (mind) [whereof the sure signs are thus α) in acquired things he rejoiceth not, β) concerning the lost, he is not worried, γ) concerning those which are to come & not yet acquired, he is affected by no disquiet] That however the saints of old have exhibited a perfect cult unto God, & that it is possible now-a-days to exhibit such to God, that is, by not serving secular (worldly) affairs, but by ruling over them, & that an holocaust perfect out of these things can be offered, I am convinced.

II. The Virtue & Efficacy of a lively Faith: Christ saith unto us, Mark 9, 23. All things are possible to him that believeth. Luke confirms 17, 6. why not therefore also rule over fleeting things? Why not also in these very matters exhibit to God a perfect service? Is the prince of this world more valiant & more powerful (potent) than Christ our Saviour & Preserver? (Has) not Paul of long-standing experience in these matters . . . having been taught thoroughly, he exclaims: I can perform all things through him that strengtheneth me (or, strengtheneth me by an inner, vital, substantial, radical force). By (with) Christ, Phil, 4, 13. as though he would say: even as without Christ I can do nothing, John 15. 5. so with Christ I can do every thing, who with express words promised: whatsoever ye shall have asked in prayer, believing, ye shall obtain, Matt. 21. 22. & that without any exception. It is not, therefore, that I shew my inability any further (more amply), since as hath been shewn, through Christ we may get all power, according to that well-known passage of John 1, 12. Whosoever, NB. whosoever indeed have received him, to those he hath given that power, to become sons of God: therefore, if (we be) sons & coheirs of all things that Christ hath, even as he himself testifieth: He that believeth on me, the same hath all things with me, or he shall even do greater things than these, John 14. 12. (the works that I do, shall he do also; &

greater works than these shall he do.) And he who shall have conquered (towards the possibility of conquering!) to him shall I give to sit with me on my throne, as I also have sat down a victor with my Father on his throne, Apoc. 3, end. And John I. Epistle, 5, 4. Whatsoever is begotten of God overcometh the world, & this is the victory, that hath overcome the world, even our Faith.

Finally, in the third place, what causes, certainly, my Pyrrhonism (skepticism) & doubting to blush, is that well-known love of perfection, with which we are bound up. Paul, describing the energy thereof, (to use an hyperbolic, though not incongruous epithet), the omnipotence in the golden to Rom. chapter 8th, finally, after a long enumeration of the parts, he exclaims: But in all these things we surpass more than we conquer, & the more so are we conquerors, through the Christ loving you. Who, therefore, in these least things, would despair of victory, as if the necessaries of life, or secular concerns, could present such obstacles unto the Christ-loving soul, that she could not please her bridegroom of the perfect? Whether or no, he who loved his own in his son before the foundation of the world, & gave to us his only begotten son, in the likeness of ourselves, unto a most ignominious death, will he, I say, donate his spirit sparingly, & imperfectly, or a spirit, inperfect, mixed, inadequate? Away with such a thought (not to say: a suspicion) of a loving soul concerning so loveworthy a God! John the Baptist eloquently testifieth the contrary of Christ: To whom, he saith, God gave spirit without measure, i. e. immeasurable & entire. He himself, of a verity, is the vine, we the branches thereof, John XV., now with what sap & spirit the vine is nourished (poured through), with the same, also, the branches (are nourished). Hence, also, concerning us Paul, Tit. 3, 6. he hath poured out his holy spirit upon us, richly, opulently, plentifully, exceeding all desire, compare Rom. 5, 5. Also, in how much we are impelled by the spirit of Christ, in so much do we bid farewell to the spirit of this world: or, in how far we love Christ, in so far do we pursue with hatred worldly & perishable things; until the *perfected love* (1 John 4, 18) thrusteth out every fear of all enemies, & the accomplisher crowneth the conquerors with a perfect crown.

But to revert to myself:

How happeneth it, my Kelpius! that unto thy God, so love-worthy, so rich, so liberal & in endless ways transcending thine every desire, in these least things, in temporal affairs, in perishable things, in foreign things, in external & transitory affairs (not to say eternal & spiritual), I say, in these thou hast not hitherto shewn the acme of perfection & scarcely shewest it even now? Knowest thou not that all the saints of old have shewn it, & art thou not very sure that it is possible even now, while the very same spirit survives, your leader, your guide, your helper & accomplisher? What sort of an account, I pray, wilt thou give, here-after, to the judge, judging without regard to persons & that according to the works of every one? To these & similar objections, I answer: Man, indeed, is born, not immediately on the first day, nor immediately in the first year, & in seven years he reaches man-hood, yet, nevertheless, man is perfect, he is furnished (endowed) with all things constituting the human body: granted, even if all the members be very delicate, & the whole body subject to various accidents, vicissitudes, sorrows & diseases: & the mind (subject to) instructions, chastisements, & exercises & an infinite number of other things: yet he despaireth not in all these, that he will once reach the age of manhood. But if these things are certain in the mortal generation, how much more (are they so) in the regenera-tion, when (where) various degrees of perfection are given. Justi-fication, namely, is accomplished through faith by one act indeed (just as the natural generation & filiation, so to speak): but renovation & sanctification are to be pursued throughout our entire lives, until we may reach the goal, i. e. the age of manhood in Christ, according to that dictum: And he that is righteous, let him do righteousness still: & he that is holy, let him be made holy still. Apoc. 22. & that well-known saying: He that doth not advance in that which is good, retrogradeth: he that doth not progress on the holy road, regresseth. Namely, even as we advance from childhood to the age of manhood, gradually, so, little by little, (we advance) from vices to virtue, &, in turn, from virtues unto virtues, 2. Pet. 1, 5. 6. 7. & Apoc. chapters I. & II. where the seven degrees; we go to the age of manhood, or the age of perfection, not in the life to come, but in this life: likewise, also, in this life, sins must be overcome; from the very bottom & the root they must be extirpated. And just as, when the sun ascendeth above the horizon, the darkness is gradually dispelled, the mists pass away by degrees; until, standing at mid-day, he triumph completely over darkness. Thus Christ, the sun & light of the spiritual & new world, not only beginneth to dispel in us the reign of darkness & foul whirlpool night, but through faith in ourselves, he conducteth the war unto perfect victory. But faith according to that passage in Paul, 1. Cor. 13, end, is of this life, not of the life to come: indeed our errors on account of the necessaries of life (of which I began speaking) belong to this life, not the future one, therefore, we must here triumph over these. Nor did the Israelites sin in that, because they did not cast out the Canaanites in one day, or in one year, but in that, they believed not the command of God nor his promise of victory, as if He were commanding impossibilities: who afterwards were willing, but in vain, because God was unwilling so I also, although I have not yet attained to thorough manhood (Ecclesiastes, 7. 29) & I have not yet cast out of my land worldly desires, & consequently not all Canaanites, yet am I daily bent upon it, that I make greater advances in the camp of the enemies, until that I may be crowned with true quietude of soul as a perfect conqueror of all enemies, having vanquished & utterly extirpated them. But if truly, according to the likeness of that worthless, cowardly & timid servant (compare Apoc. 21, 8., Matt. 25), I should despair in this life of the gain (advantage) & the victory, & should accuse the Lord, as if He were commanding impossibilities, of severity, I should not obey His command of perfection, Matt. 5, 48. of perfect sanctification, Lev. 11, 44. chapter 19, 2. 1. Pet. 1, 15, 16. I should distrust Him, He offering aid & victory, I should delay the war against the enemies, assailing me in this present world, to the future world, where no enemies are given; I say by doing this, I should sin, & deservedly would I be hurled at last into the lowermost darkness, inasmuch as I, who would not go out during the six days (as those would not, who were idle), i. e. in this life, I would seek the manna on the Sabbath day, i. e., in the life to come.

I have rested with the foolish virgins, the bridegroom having entered, & the gates having been closed, I was knocking, i. e. in this life, as if it were night, I neglected to walk in the perfect light of Christ, & the like of her I went about the will-o'-the-wisp, but I did not go forth to meet him a-shouting with the prudent ones, while it was midnight as yet, & the gate open, & the bridegroom was coming on. In this manner I should be like a child, who, if he were to reach manhood hereafter, should foreknow how great hardships were yet to be overcome with great pain, to obtain wherewith he should be fed & clothed, how great annoyances were to be undergone at the schools, & chastisements to be sustained for cultivating the mind towards the acquisition of prudence in concerns of business: I say, considering (weighing) thoroughly these & other grievances of that sort, he should despair of obtaining virile age in this life, & place his trust in death, as if dead, he should at least come off a perfect man. But dropping this fool, I have chosen to imitate the infant Redeemer, who grew both in age & wisdom before God & men: this one remained hidden from the twelfth year of his age for eighteen years. He remained hidden, I say, but he lived well, i. e. he grew from day to day, until he went forth, in his thirtieth year, *A Man*. And, after that, he most perfectly fulfilled the will of his Father for the salvation of the entire world, he went out of this life, &, sitting at the right hand of his omnipotent Father, he sendeth his Holy Spirit unto all believing on him. He also aideth mine infirmities; for me & in me he pleadeth with unspeakable sighing (Rom. 8, 26) & he accomplisheth in me, that I am both willing & at times thoroughly do the will of my Father Abba. And so the virtue of the Almighty is perfected in mine infirmity.

I believe, therefore, according to the testimony of the entire Scripture with all Saints: *That our Father wisheth, wisheth, I say, that his children be free from every fault: that God wisheth they may withhold themselves from every sin; mankind were created by Him for justice, & He donated them with the spirit of His Son. That Christ desireth that those be purified from every sin, for the expiation of whom, he himself became a victim, & that the virgin soul is to be delivered up to him; a virgin, I say, chaste & devoid of every wrinkle or vice, he entrusted her unto us. That the Holy Spirit effecteth that this will of the Father & of the Son be accomplished in us as yet in this life.* And, although, thus far I may have been subjected to infinite temptations & may have borne my cross daily, nor have always advanced with equal steps, nay rather have fallen oftentimes, & as to that, into the horrid whirlpool & filthy mire (Psalm XL. 3.) & have drawn near the gate of death (Psalm IX.), insomuch that with the same David, I should have cried out: (Psalm 38.) *Jehovah, turn not upon me fiercely! Punish me not in thine anger!* [This chastisement may be of the healing not of the killing one: with the rod of love of a father toward his son, Hebr. 12., not of a judge pursuing with the sword of judgment]. *For thy darts are thrust upon me, thy hand presseth me down* [& with Job, chap. 6. *The arrows of the Almighty are within me, the poison whereof my spirit drinketh up, while I am wrestling with the terrors of God.*] Thy chastisement in my heart, the continued representation of Thy dreadful judgment, & the long lasting absence of Thy gratuitous consolations, bringeth it about, that I begin to perceive nothing if not (only) sin within me & without. *For nothing is sound in my body* [viciousness dwelleth in me! for I know & daily experience that the good dwelleth not in me, i. e. in my flesh or in the human nature; but sin dwelleth in me, against this] so great is Thine anger, that Thou didst not spare Thy son, who was a stranger to sin, but didst give him over into death, & madest an execration for execrable me, that I too may become ingrafted in that similitude of his death, to the end that the sinful body may be cast off, nor that I be in bondage of sin any longer, for in my limbs there is nothing uninjured on account of my sin.

VI.

LETTER TO MARY ELIZABETH GERBER IN VIRGINIA.

To Mary Elizabeth Gerber in Virginia,

(*Translation.*)

October 8th, 1704.

Contents:—An answer to her letter, in which she requests an expression of my opinion concerning the Quakers.

Immanuel! Granted the request. Eph. 1, 17–23. In Jesu C., our Lord, most esteemed & revered Sister:

YOUR beloved missive of Aug. 23rd '4, duly received. I rejoice in that you would awake from the death-like slumber of sin of the world, & from worldly sentiments, & in that you earnestly covet the inheritance of the Saints, & would walk in the light of the Son of God. I, likewise, entertain the confident hope, that the God of Peace, hath, indeed, begun in your soul the work of the new creation (regeneration), & will, through the blood of the everlasting Covenant, also, perfect the same unto the day of Jesu Christ. As regards other matters, & them also (the Friends?) (less scattered in the communities of the present day, & in spirit bound, expecting the hope of Sion) (Zion) these let us carry in our hearts, for God, & pray for them—your love requesteth of me, all manner of experience & cognition, to the end that you may prove, *what be the best;* especially in these latter, dangerous times, in which not only the mockers (scoffers), described by the Apostles (2. Pet. 3, 3.2. Tim. 3, 1) do in all stations of life & in all religions so prodigiously increase, but also there have gone forth all manner of angels & spirits (1 John 4.7.2. Pet. 2, 1. Matth. 24.

11. 1. Cor. 11. 19. 1. Tim. 4. 1.) & they have instituted congregations, one arming against the other. Here Temples of the
Lord! Here the Catholic Church of Christ! Here the Orthodox
Evangelical! Here the Chosen Reformed! Here the again-born
baptized (Anabaptists?)! Here the Folk (People) of God, walking in the Light, etc. Now some of these have their distinct praise,
gift of beauty, strength, might, power, wisdom, order, light &c., the
which, indeed, are apparent to an impartial eye, whilst at the same
time, we perceive, that they have received said ornaments but piece-
meal, & not in the highest & most irrefragable perfection: the one
hath received this, the other that, none (not one) of them hath
received all (ornaments) alone in the highest degree: all in part,
not one in united harmony. One possesseth something apart from
the rest & very similar to the image of perfection, which is wanting
to the other, the latter, in turn, hath something, that is wanting to
the former, &c. Howbeit every one vaunteth as being the best &
most comely amongst all these women, & the last (of which you,
dear Sister, write) claims to be the only dove, dearest unto her
mother, yea, the chosen one of her mother, yea, verily, the mother
or the very self of the New Jerusalem. But unto this very day are
not agreed amongst themselves, *as to which of them deserveth the
chief place:* yet why speak of their reaching an agreement? They
have no such intention: they even contend among themselves, but
not as did erstwhile the Disciples of Christ, as to who should be
regarded chief in the Mystery of Grace (devotion), but which of
them be most accomplished in the mystery of malice, the arch
heretic, yea, even the Babylonian harlot herself: nor are they content with reviling, those that are in power use the sword, those
lacking the sword make swords of their tongues, & with such blind
rage, that it moves to pity; first, that they are unable to recognize
themselves; second, nor those against whom they are fighting;
thirdly, least of all are they aware of what they profess (this is
especially true of the last).

"Who are they, pray?" You, esteemed Sister, will probably
ask, & how shall I learn to know them, that I may not err in my

judgment, & become a partaker of their contention, & come into
danger of the judgment, that needs must follow? " Answer: This
is taught by Paul, Gal. 4. Coloss. 2., by the Apocalypse & by the
Song of Songs of Sol., as followeth, namely: *They all are sisters
amongst themselves & children of Jerusalem, but not of her that is
free, but of her that is a handmaid & in thraldom with her children.* Which becometh clear (see p. 9. 10. Gal. 4), that they all
serve weak & paltry tenets (statutes). They observe days &
months & feasts & seasons, each in his particular manner & differently, as compared with the others, (hence the origin of the strife,
schism or sects among them). Yet in this they are all agreed,
that they *serve* their own tenets, which they love, & which they
recognize as good & true; these tenets they exalt, defend, propa-
gate, & extol before others (proselytize), etc. All of which
(sects, etc.) (however profligate some of them may be) have a
semblance of wisdom & truth; wherefore, also, Paul calleth all
such tenet-service or living according to law—" Philosophy " or
love of wisdom, Col. 2. Of these (people) they teach in the
schools of the present day, of each distinctly, as well as of what
truth they hold, so far as demonstrable in Holy Writ, but the body
or the entity herself & the occult wisdom & truth are not therein
(in these meetings), but in Christ, in whom there lie hidden all
treasures of wisdom & understanding, yea the entire plenitude of
the Deity dwelleth corporally in Him. Through Him we are
rendered entirely participant of the entity of all tenets deduced
from (mentioned in) Holy Writ. (As Paul adduceth a renowned
example of circumcision, Col. 2, V. 11), but such tenets as are
not mentioned in the Scriptures, these appertain (are referable) to
mankind, commandments & doctrines; Vol. 2. 22. N.B. Matth.
15. 9. Isaiah (Esa) 29. 13. unto which, indeed, some of these
church-women do more homage than to those, which are called the
" shadows of the body " by Paul, Col. 2. 17. Hebr. 8. 5. chap.
10. 1. Whereby they are clearly recognized, of what mind they
be, namely, children of Sinai or Hagar, of the bond-woman & not
of the free understanding, yea of Sinai, even of his great splendor,

light, spirit, clearness, enlightenment, mutes etc. Especially in the New Testament, far more splendidly than in the Old, in which it is more spiritual: Thus it is ... wherefore, up to this time, naught else hath appeared in Christendom (primitive Christianity excepted); for what of Zion hath been there & still abideth, is only in the desert, whereof we shall soon speak more amply; hence it hath come to pass, that many a one, inexperienced in the word of justice, & that such, whose senses were not practiced in discriminating, have honored the bond-woman, instead of the woman (mistress) herself, &, likewise, regarded the bond-slave for the Son. To the end that you, esteemed Sister, may not fall into the same error, I shall briefly touch upon what is meant by the Woman, the free and only Dove of the rightful Solomon, or the New Jerusalem, so that, by comparing the one with the other, you may recognize both more readily. Isaiah saith, chap. 65, that in the New Jerusalem, which the Lord willed to create on earth (N.B. on earth, &, therefore, not in heaven, though she descendeth from heaven) the voice of lamentation & of weeping shall be heard no more. Likewise saith He in the Apocalypse, chap. 21. 4. death shall be no more, nor sorrow, nor wailing (crying), nor pains. But whereof doth a repentant heart complain & weep more, than of sin? What else is the sting of death, than sin? What filleth us with greater grief, than sin committed? Where is the loudest wailing & the greatest pain, if not in the anxiety of being born again (regeneration), John 16.21. Hence, the sense hereof is: In the New Jerusalem there shall be no more sinners, none that stand in need of repentance, none that suffer the pains of regeneration: (as we read in the last verse: Naught that is vile shall enter therein, nor that worketh abomination & falsehoods), but regenerated ones only, holy, just, new men, who can sin no more, 1 John 3.9. chap. 8, 10. Heb. 9.28., who, therefore, die no more, neither bodily nor spiritually, Apoc. 21, 4. 1 Cor. 15, 26. 54. John 11. 26. Luke, 20. 36. In brief: The curse and death, which are laid in & upon the entire creation (creature), by the fall of the first Adam, under which even to this hour all creatures have groaned, Rom. 8, 18–25. shall be completely removed by the atonement & efficacy of the everlasting redemption in the blood of the second Adam, offered up on the cross, when He shall come a second time bodily (I say bodily, because some would have it but spiritually, whereas it shall be both; still, however, it is only in the mystery of devotion as yet see A.A. 1, 10.2. (acts of Apostles) Thess. 5, 10. that He appear glorious in & with His Saints & wonderful in & with (thus readeth the original text) all the faithful, which Paul, Rom. 8. calleth the manifestation of the children of God. Who are the children of the resurrection, Luke, 20. 36. This shall be the year of the great jubilee, when all prisoners will be set free, & each one will return to his parental inheritance, the which we have lost in our first father Adam, whereof the entire Old Testament is filled. Of this the Apostles & first Christians had but the firstlings, but not the fullness, not the perfection (Rom. 8. 23) (Cor. 13, 9–2 Cor. 5. 7.) the which they awaited, as they had, indeed, so plentifully received the coming (future) of Christ in the spirit, as no congregation or church after Him even to this hour. They possessed all manner of spiritual gifts both for their inner glorification, as well as for the outer working of miracles. Thus, in their community, there was not heard any longer the voice of groaning, weeping & lamentation, but that of joy & rejoicing (1 A. 2, 46. 47. C. 3, 31. Rom. 5, 3–5. Phil. 4, 4. 1 Pet. 4. 13). If an unclean one, or a *hypocrite* or a liar wanted to join them, he either was liable to instant death, or he was punished in the presence of ALL, & the hidden things of his heart became manifest, so that he had to fall upon his countenance (prone) & adore God & confess that God was truly in him. 1 Cor. 4, 24, 25. (though these did not long enjoy their happiness, for the great apostasy & Antichrist was up already and doing in their days. Thess. 2, 7.) And yet they became not prouder & filled, as though they had enough already & wanted no more (as in Laod. Apoc. 3) for they had seized (grasped) the utmost dove-like simplicity, the which alone seeketh the King's heart, that is not satisfied with any gifts, until that she have the Giver himself, (not to say (much less) that she loveth the Giver for the sake of the gifts) but to exclaim all along: Come, Lord Jesu! yea, the Spirit himself & the bride said, Come! And he that beareth witness of all this, saith: yea, I come quickly! amen. Whence all, that are participant of the same Spirit cry, by day & by night, at all places, whithersoever they have been scattered: " Yes, come Lord Jesu! " And, pray, dear Sister, how can the bride be prepared without the bridegroom? Or, is the perfection to be wrought in the spirit only? But then, what of the resurrection from death & the redemption of this body, for which all members of Christ do, with Paul, so anxiously cry (Rom. 8, 15. Phil. 2, 20. 21. 1 Cor. 15. entirely. Col. 3, 4. 1 John 3, 2. 2. Peter 3. entirely. 2. Cor. 5, 1–11.) Did Christ, then, in spirit only ascend into heaven? &, hence, is He to be expected in spirit only? Shall the selfsame Jesus, whom his disciples did see to ascend bodily, from the Mount of Olives come back again, just as his disciples saw Him ascending into heaven: why, then, do our Laodiceans of the present day declare, that He hath (is) come already? *" He is come," they say* (as I myself have heard and read in their writings). *" He is come, Friends, we bide none other! "* Is, then, he, whom the Apostles & primitive Christians waited for, an other one, than he, whom they had (seen) already ascend, & who sent them from heaven after ten days the promise of the Father, namely: The Holy Spirit? Or, did they await Him merely for these ten days, but not thereafter, because they now had His spirit? Why, then, as aforesaid, do the spirit himself & the bride, at the conclusion of the Apocalypse, cry: " Come, Lord Jesu! "

Yes, dear Friends! If He be come & ye bide none other, why, then, do we hear at all your meetings, especially when these are most godly, as you say, the voice of sobbing, of weeping, lamentation, yea anguish, sorrow, pain & ululation as for one dead? Is this the jubilant voice of the bride for her bridegroom? If, however, ye do rejoice by virtue of being moved by His Spirit as the (since) Spirit of Christ is made manifest among you at times, just as amongst all other congregations) O, then, do for once give

5

honor unto God & confess: *that you have, indeed, received a glimpse of His beauty through His spirit in your hearts, but never yet have ye seen the Lord of Glory himself with His royal diadem, wherewith His Mother shall crown Him on the day of His exaltation!* Or, had ye seen Him, your heart would rejoice in so much, that your joy would nevermore be taken from you (John 16, 22), since, as you say, you must at every meeting await Him anew. Yea, if ye had but His spirit, the other Paraclete, whom the Father giveth that He remain supreme (John 14, 16), remaining and dwelling in you, ye would not begin to rejoice as at a marriage feast for the time, but with the woman in the desert & her seed, together with the Spirit, ye would cry day and night: " Come, Lord Jesu! " & patiently await His coming. But if ye be the holy people, God's only people, whence cometh it, that the number of the uncircumcised, of the unclean, of the abominable & horrid liars, & of all manner of sinners, is far greater among you, than the number of the just? Have not your tenets (statutes), symbols or sacraments, whereby ye are distinguished from other communities, become, at present, the pall of (for) vices, under cover of which the worst hypocrites can conceal, yea really do conceal themselves? Saith old George Fox in his Journal: *As soon as any statute, though it be the way of the Apostles, hath become a cloak for hypocrites, they are an abomination before God.* Now, should I consider your society the most beautiful among women, that is free from blemish & hereditary evil, Cant. 4. 10., as the community of the first-born, begotten in the perfection of justice? Alas, ye are not even like unto the community of the Apostles & first Christians, who were but a picture & a shadow of the future (community) ! How could ye be the (community) of which they (Apostles & first Christians) prophesied, & for whose manifestation they did so earnestly pray? The best among you must work out their salvation with fear & trembling. Now, the spirit of fear & trembling is the spirit of Hagar & Sinai, Heb. 12, 21. & not the spirit of Hagar & Sarah, which is the spirit of the new creation in the new Adam, Jesus, the Mediator & Founder of the new covenant, & (the spirit) crieth: Abba, Father, Rom. 8, 15. Gal. 4, 6. & worketh in us a *perfect love,* which expelleth fear, 1 John 4, 18. & (is) a joy on the day of Judgment, as is (felt) by those who have penetrated from death unto life, John 5, 24. (Concerning this joyous confidence & assurance, read Rom. 8. 31–39., which are wrought by the spirit of mercy (grace) & faith, (which proceedeth) from Zion & the Glad Tidings, which (spirit) gladdeneth the heart & maketh it to feel gay towards God & man, so that we will, without compulsion, willingly & gladly, do good unto all men, suffer all things, serve every one, &c. But the servile spirit of Sinai is for ever complaining, mourning, murmuring, anguishing & tormenting the conscience forever more, & yet being unable to help, nor yet to impart strength, since always vexing). Now ye have, indeed, caught a glimpse (of the true community, but deeming the same endangered as yet & fixing a limit (measure), therefore you give those coming (to you) opportunely, to understand that ye have as yet not reached the tranquilly flowing nether waters of perfection because these are inexhaustible (lost in inexhaustibility) —But, esteemed Sister, I seem to have forgotten you, in apostrophizing (addressing) others, while writing to you. But may the Lord give unto (you) her the spirit of Wisdom & Scrutiny, so that she may, with Mary, choose the best part. But methinks I hear her say: This would I fain (have) should I forget thee, Jerusalem, may my right be forgotten. My tongue must cleave unto my palate, whenever I suffer not, Jerusalem, thy memory to be my greatest joy. This is the free one! This is the fairest amongst women. This is the dove, the only one of her mother, the dearest, the chosen one of her mother. But, alas, where is she! Who leadeth me unto her! Since my former leaders have been but misleaders, & those that offered oil unto me, were the petty merchants in Chaldea. Tell me, where He pastureth, whom my soul loveth, where He resteth on the noon-day of His greatest power, that I may but wander to & fro among the herds of His companions! Where, pray, is the fairest of women, so that I may not become enamored of one of the women, described above, & be contaminated by her.

Hath (is) the only dove, indeed, flown heavenward, or, if she be as yet on earth, tell me, in which forest she resteth, and in which city am I to find her abode? The answer is: She is, indeed, as yet on earth, & she was glorious to behold in the days of the Apostles. But, after she had given birth to the self-same boy, she fled into the desert (wilderness). Apoc. 12., whence she shall soon ascend, leaning upon her friend. Cant. 8, 5. (Song of Songs). And when she shall see the above-mentioned daughters, then will she carefully prove them; the queens themselves & the concubines will praise her. Cant. 6, 8. (9). Meseemeth, however, I hear my esteemed Sister say: "This answer is too obscure (dark); I can not understand it. Describe unto me the dove in her true form, & her feathers, so that I may know her. Yes, tell me, without concealing anything, her place of abode; for I shall not cease from seeking, until that I may have found her, though it should be at the price of my goods & blood, yea, though it cost me my life." Answer: May the Lord strengthen her in her resolution, & vouchsafe that this zeal may nevermore become extinguished in her, but ever burn brightly! I, in proportion to my slight ability, shall gladly do my best. Nevertheless, I must, esteemed Sister, overtly tell her; that we can neither find nor know this dove, *except we ourselves become as doves,* &, as soon as we be such, forthwith we fly into the wilderness to join the other. This wisdom was not concealed from David; hence his yearning, Psalm 55. 7. 8. Would that I had wings as doves, that I might fly & perchance remain! Lo, then would I fly afar off & lodge in the wilderness. Selah. But whoso desire to fly, if he fly not well, will inevitably plunge himself into danger, wherein many a soul perisheth. Therefore, the Lord saith in Isaiah c. 30, 15. N.B. Jer. 14, 10.

If ye remained still, ye would be aided; by being quiet & by hoping, ye would be strong. Hence they chatter only & mourn with Isaiah (38, 15. c. 59, 11.) as a dove day & night. And when their eyes have become as doves' eyes, Cant. 1, 15. c. 4, 1. they look only at their beloved & hide themselves in His wounds, as in the clefts of the rock, Cant. 2, 14. To the end that they may not, like the foolish & decoyed (or timid, without heart) dove Ephraim, now invoke Egypt, & then run to Assyria, Hosea 7, 11., imploring of these spiritual, of those corporal (bodily) food & aid, for there be dove-vendors as well as oil-vendors, to whom the silly doves & virgins run. Oh, he that rightly knoweth these, in verity doth he beware of them. The oil signifieth the *Spirit,* the dove, the proper form of the bride of the lamb, which is *love.* Thus there are to be noted especially, according to the number of the five prudent & five foolish virgins, five things, that our five senses be not injured in their maidenly, dovelike simplicity in Christ, 2, Cor. 11, 3. Matth. 10. 16., namely: 1. The bridegroom, 2. the virgins, 3. the vendors, 4. the oil, 5. the lamps. But, may God give her the understanding of the spirit of Jesu Christ, that she, according to the admonition of Paul, 2. Tim. 2, 15. may rightfully divide the word of truth, &, after she have flown from the filth of the world by the knowledge (recognition) of the Crucified for her sin, 2. Pet. 2, 20. nor, indeed, purchase the oil or light herself for the bridegroom; nor forthwith regard some, though they have oil in their lamps, as prudent virgins, because these also have arisen at midnight of the great schism (falling off), & will testify to the universal slumber in sin of the world. Verily, the vendors sit not only at Rome & in the great church, where, alas, God have mercy! there is little oil, but, indeed, a great, yea Egyptian & palpable darkness. Even the little foxes spoil the vineyard, even men catch & kill the doves.

Should the virgins that are cleansed (washed off) by the blood of the lamb, from the temeration of (with) their first woman (wife), Apoc. 1, 5. chap. 7, 14. & who now follow the lamb, Apoc. 14, 4., again be defiled with other women, because these may be more comely (beautiful) than the first? Let that (thought) be far removed! Those, however, that do it, will, in time, find their second purification more difficult than the first.

Now, my dear Sister might say, "Even so would I, as a chaste, pure virgin, follow the lamb, the spotless, the pure, even the lamb of God, slain for us, whithersoever it goeth, because I, too, have been ransomed by it. But how am I to walk, in this Sardian dispersion, among so many church women, that I may not soil nor bedraggle my garments, Rev. 3, 4. c. 14, 4.?" Answer: If she be really in earnest, & if she be conscious of a manly, strong & genuine (uncolored) *love* in her to Jesus & His bride, yea, if such a *simple love,* which hateth duplicity, Mar. 6, 24. 2. Cor. 6, 14, 15. 1. John 2. 15. Gal. 1, 10. Jac. 4, 4. If she find, I say, this love in her, or at least an essential longing thereafter, to the end that this love may once be perfected in her, & she be rooted in & founded upon this love, Eph. 3, 17. Is it thus? Come on! She is rapt of the dove-kind! Nothing can harm her so long as she abide therein, if she herself forfeit not this love, either, 1. *By slighting the same:* or, 2. By breaking forth too early. In order to prevent this the only mean is, to fly into the desert on eagle's wings, where, even now, the woman, the bride of the lamb, is most assuredly nourished unto her time appointed (which is very nigh at hand) after the expiration of which, she will break forth, first, as the dawn, afterwards, fair as the moon, then, chosen as the sun, but finally, terrible as vanguards of hosts, Cant. 6, 9. "O yes! would she say, whoso would rightly understand this all, to be preserved from the dragon!"

But, dear Soul! pray do not entertain melancholy thoughts concerning these subjects, nor imagine strange things, for in *virginal love,* all things are contained. If she in childlike simplicity weigh and consider all that I have already said, I do not doubt, but that God will vouchsafe prosperity (thrivingness). But, if she understand all in its first sense, then, God be praised, & may He grant the will & the accomplishment. But, if not? Then, let her be patient, & make no ado, for the time might come, when it would be serviceable unto her. I must now hasten towards the conclusion, yet it will not, as I hope, be disagreeable, if I talk a little more about the wilderness. This is twofold: 1. Corporal & 2. Spiritual. In the corporal sense, there are again two divisions (yet this sense is unfathomable). Herein it signifieth those who fled into the wilderness before the great apostasy (falling off), soon after the times of the Apostles (whereof the life of the primitive fathers (forefathers) is worthy of perusal). Whereof in Rev. c.12ψλ to 6. verse 2. Here, the corporeal wilderness of the entire Christianity, that hath fallen off (apostatized), is meant, which is called the great city of Babylon & Egypt, in which the woman, that is, all the true members of Christ & children of the higher (upper) Jerusalem are hidden, amongst all religions & stations in life, as well as excluded, Apoc. 12. at the end (for desert signifieth as much as " hidden " or not manifest). Therefore, we ought not to despise any religion, because Christ still hath in all His true members; nor must we regard any religion too high, as hath been said above sufficiently. The spiritual sense, however, though it, too, is inexhaustible, may be subdivided into two heads: 1. In regard to the whole community or body of Christ, which we shall, for the present, not discuss, 2. With regard to every member of this body in particular. Just as now the entire body of Christ is in the desert or hidden, so also is every member or soul in particular. No reasoning, though it put on all spectacles, can recognize the latter, yet may be angered at them, & will take counsel to extirpate these hidden ones of the Lord, Psalm 83, 4. Coloss. 3, 3. But the Lord hideth himself secretly in his tent (pavilion). But as regards the actual state of a soul in the wilderness, I cannot at present describe. If She, dear soul! become rightly participant of the dove-kind, she will, as aforesaid, also obtain eagle's wings to fly thereinto. Then will she *experience,* what it be, to chatter (coo) as a lonely turtledove, day and night for the longed for loved one, how, meanwhile, the loved one feed her with the hidden manna, Apoc. 2, 7. How He will let her know the secret & hidden wisdom, Psalm 5, 8. Psalm 28, 14 . . . which God ordained (prescribed) before the world . . . splendor. How He will donate unto her His great, secret goods (treasures), which are better than life, Psalm 31, 20. How He will teach her to know the hidden God & Saviour, who leadeth His saints so wonderfully, Isaiah 45, 15. & the Father who seeth in secret Matth. 6, 6. She will experience, how this friend of her soul sweeten the bitter waters of tribulations and sufferings in march through the wood of life & mild yoke of His cross, Exod. 15. Matth. 11.

How the hard rock in Horeb becomes (is transformed into) a fresh fountain of the water of life by knocking with faith, Exod. 17, 1. Cor. 10, 4. How during the day, from out the cloud that guideth her, so many droplets of grace (mercy) of heavenly dew, will fall upon her as a baptism of grace. This will be unto her a day of joy & shouting, when the Holy Ghost shall stir in her heart & move the waters, so that the fount shall be poured forth from out her eyes in tears of pure joy. Oh, blessed baptism of water! Who would not daily, yea, hourly, be baptized thus! But there followeth also a night upon this day, wherein the fiery column, as God in the east, will preserve her, which is the baptism in fire of the Son, until that, at last, the old birth, bred in Egypt, and longing for the Egyptian pots of lust, shall completely die out together with Moses. Then will the true Jonah-Jesus lead the *new birth,* that was born in the desert, & is now grown to the age of manhood, then will he lead this birth to the taking of the new Canaan, yea, lead her thereinto. Oh, who would not long for this desert (wilderness)! which is so joyful, & standeth so gladsome & bloometh as the lilies! Yes, it bloometh and standeth rejoicing, for the splendor of Lebanon is given unto her (the wilderness). The ornament (excellency) of Carmel & Saron (Sharon), Isaiah, 35, 1. Even the most bitter myrrhs here contain the most hidden sweetness. Even the heaviest burthen is light, & the hardest yoke is mild (gentle). The deepest sadness hath hidden in itself, the inmost joy; darkness is as light, Psalm 139, 12. Here, dying is to become alive; poverty is the greatest wealth; hunger & thirst are as the most longed for food & most refreshing drink; to be nothing and to become nothing, is to inherit all things; to have nothing is to possess all things; to be weak, is the greatest strength; unrest is the securest peace; no trouble, no work tires, for the more one works, the stronger one becomes, & yet the feeblest weakness hath hidden in itself the greatest strength. From out such desert there shall arise (be built) the fairest city, namely, the New Jerusalem. Now, then, Esteemed Sister, are you willing to come into the wilderness, & are ye pleased to flee thereinto? Then it is necessary to understand these things spiritually & not corporally, because all things gross be herein. Be their names what they will, there are no wildernesses in the primitive (first) spiritual understanding, but inhabited cities, full of temples & altars. If she be willing to follow the lamb, whithersoever it goeth, then let her not follow the women, because one is only contaminated with these. Wouldst thou convert thyself, then convert thyself unto me, saith the Lord, Jer. 4, 1. If she have the spirit of the Lord as her teacher & master, she must, indeed, be very desirous (studious) if she be not content with Him. But if she hear Him in a friend of the bridegroom, He will always direct her to the lamb, as John, & bid neither himself, nor any one else to follow. But he that followeth after the lamb, must not run before it, lest the wolf catch him. To follow Him is the surest way; to remain with Him is the best security; & on His pasture there is found the best food. And this she may do, if she, according to His own admonition, Matth. 6, 6. remain at home, bodily & spiritually, go into her chamber, lock the door, & pray to her Father in secret, & her Father, who seeth in secret, will reward her openly. Amen.

With cordial greetings, I am ever ready to serve you in Christ, & I shall be happy to hear that you are prospering. The Lord, our King, grant her His benison from Zion, to the end that she may see Jerusalem, her salvation, throughout her life.

J. KELPIUS.

P.S. Many more things could I write, but, how is it possible to describe the inexpressible with pen & ink! The Lord, however, unite our hearts by His spirit, that we, in united harmony, may grow together in one faith & knowledge of the Son of God, & ever become a more perfect man, who is to be in the measure of the perfect age of Christ (see Eph. 4, 14, 15, 16). Thus we shall, though absent in body, in the selfsame spirit be present one to another & offer up one & the same petition, prayer, intercession & thanksgiving through the hand of the Mediator J. C. ———— H.

Buntchÿ sends his best regards. Both he & H. Mattheÿ rejoice exceedingly because of her conversion to (growth in) Christ. These men came to us about a year ago, & have, in this short time, increased powerfully in the renunciation of the cares of this world & the allurements thereof. May the Lord strengthen & confirm these dear souls furthermore. They live amongst us, less scattered, & with us, they long, that, indeed, our Arch-Shepherd would bring together the scattered children of God through the power (by virtue) of His suffering (passion). (John 11, 52). Jerusalem, indeed, is being built in this sorrowful time, whilst we hold the stones wrought with the one hand, & hold the weapon in the other, Nehem. 4, 17. And the stones, each one for itself are prepared outside of Jerusalem. Those that are perfected await the perfection of the rest, in whom the corner-stone himself, the first-born, our Immanuel, doth wait, Heb. 10, 13.

Whence the long-suffering of the great Architect, our God, yea, of our Father in Christ becomes apparent, who causeth our brethren, afore perfected toward salvation—to wait, that they might not be perfected without us, Heb. 11, 40. When, however, the last stone shall have been perfected, then will the edifice suddenly appear without stroke of hammer, without tumult & shouting, appear in its divine splendor, beauty & magnificence. Therefore, beloved soul, let us patiently (meekly) suffer chastening, to the end that we obtain His sanctification (whereof read Heb. 12.) without which no one shall see God. In my epistle I have answered her request to a sufficiency, but hath it been to her edification? Should be pleased to hear hereof. But, if she find therein ought that may cause her some doubt, scruple, or the like, or be it that aught may be too obscure or unintelligible, yea, if she would know aught more, I am, as a fellow-servant, ready to serve her according to the ability which God granteth. For it also pleaseth God to work even by means (& indeed, oftentimes by very weak ones, of which I am probably one of the most inconsiderable). Just as He hath done by your soul through one dear friend Chawiley (?) though he is joined unto a certain congregation, nevertheless he hath somewhat of the universal charity (love), whereof for the present (I will speak no more)—thus he hath been instrumental, largely, to the first awakening of her soul. But now, may the faithful Arch-Shepherd & Bishop (Overseer) of our salvation give her His spirit Himself towards a union (a growth or growing to) & complete perfection. Amen.

I remain, Esteemed Sister,

Your faithful brother, J. K.

BOOK PLATE OF BENJAMIN FURLEY, THE ROTTERDAM MERCHANT.

VII.

LETTER TO DR. JOHANNES FABRICIUS (ALTDORFINUS), GERMANY.

To Dr. Fabricius, Prof. Theol. at Helmstadt:

July 23rd, 1705.

YOUR Magnificence:—The joy your letter afforded me I am unable, at present, to describe. I did behold in it, as in a mirror, the sincerity and uprightness of my good old master, Dr. Fabricius. What dear Mr. Ingelstaetter, evrettore dei Falkein, reported, is true, so far as appertaineth to the principal point, namely, that I have not become a Quaker. Such an idea hath never come into my mind, albeit I love them from my inmost soul, even as I do all other sects that approach and call themselves Christ's, the Baptists even not excluded, and, with Peter, I have found out, in deed and truth, that God regardeth not the person, but in all sorts of work and religion. He that feareth Him, and doeth what is right, is agreeable to Him. I could report of magnalities (if space permitted) which this great God hath wrought even amongst the Indians, whereof there is some printed notice in the Memoirs of the Phil. Soc. in London, and how they are brought to grief now and then by blind-mouthed Christians. Yet one instance I will report, as abashed Sir W. Penn, when he was here last, Anno 1701 (if I remember rightly) when he wanted to preach to them of faith in the God of Heaven and Earth, at their Kintika (thus they call their festivity). After having listened to him with great patience; they answered: "You bid us believe in the Creator and Preserver of Heaven and Earth, though you do not believe in Him yourself, nor trust in Him. For you have now made your own the

D.JOANNES FABRICIVS
Altdorfinus

PORTRAIT OF MAGISTER FABRICIUS.

TUTOR AND FRIEND OF KELPIUS.

FROM AN OLD COPPERPLATE AT HELMSTADT.

land we held in common amongst ourselves and our friends. You now take heed, night and day, how you may keep it, so that no one may take it from you. Indeed, you are anxious even beyond your span of life, and divide it among your children. This manor for this child, that manor for that child. But we have faith in God the Creator and Preserver of Heaven and Earth. He preserveth the sun, He hath preserved our fathers so many moons (for they count not by years). He preserveth us, and we believe and are sure that He will also preserve our children after us, and provide for them, and because we believe this, we bequeath them not a foot of land." Whenever we shall be made worthy to see the many and varied dwellings in our Father's house (for who would be so simple, to say these dwellings were all of one sort), it is my belief we shall then see that the same Architect cared little about our common formula and systematic architecture. And, I trow, many disciples of Moses and Christ, when in want or dying, might be glad if they shall be received in any of the huts, described above, by him, whom they perhaps accused of heresy in this life. I hope that God, who maketh happy both man and beast, and hath mercy on all his children, will, at last, make all men, as died in Adam, alive in the other. But life and death are further distinguished from change, so that those that have been made to live in Christ, must be delivered from the second death. I know that some cranks, spiriti Divines, trouble and crucify themselves concerning this Lexion theologiae (as they call it), but especially the Reprobratites, because these (Restitution of all things) cancel and crucify their dogmas so very frequently. Meseems, however, their little faith hath its origin in the misunderstanding of the word Eternity, which neither in Greek nor in Hebrew denoteth a time but an end, but rather the contrary as they have both singular and plural numbers, and Paul even speaketh of the birth of Eternities. But just as the luminaries of the firmament are the dimensions of our time, so it seemeth that the Eternities have, also, their dimensions, which, however, those (sensual Man's having not the spirit) cannot well see, wherefore allowance must be made, if they, perchance, judge hereof as the blind do of colors. But if the Lord from out his infinite plentitude should give them the spiritual mind, they will, no doubt, judge otherwise. How wroth I formerly would wax toward those who would not accept the sayings of Schertzer or Calov as Oracles. And I trust in the infinite mercy of God (and your Magnificence also had great patience with me and to me, indeed, publicly, whereof I have since often been ashamed, but admired your Magnificence's humility and prudence), why should I then look with evil eye upon my blind neighbor, because God hath, perchance, showed me beforehand the abundance of His Mercy, by opening mine eyes before theirs? Not to speak of, that I see but little fragments of the fragmentary work and the men of the creation as trees! But, especially, because I hope to become one in God through Christ both with those who do not yet see as I do, and with those that see much better and farther than I.

Although I proffer this common love in the brotherly love, yet the brotherly love, the Philadelphiae, remains with me on a firm foundation; whence I was wronged, if I have been called a Quaker on account of the former (common love), or even furthermore, a Papist, as has been done by the Quakers in this country, as I was unwilling to enter the married state, however advantageous the connection, wherefore I was either a Jesuit or an Indian Deitist, although, by the grace of God, it is easy for me to be judged from a human standpoint. Nevertheless I have mercy on such untimely judges and condemners who are oblivious of the express prohibition of Christ and Paul, though professing to be his disciples; Therefore I can harmonize as little with the canon of the Anglical Church (Confession), as with the anathema of the Council of Trent, though having no part in the errors mentioned. To the honor of the Anglical Church, I must confess, that they practice the Doctrine of universal grace much better than the Lutherans. Their 39 Theses, or Articles (I had almost said 40 less one) are so mild and general, that they can be accepted by any one, who is not too narrow-minded and of too little faith. If anyone amongst them have but a private view, as, for instance, concerning the universal restitution, the Millennium, the Metemptosis, etc., he is, on that account, not excommunicated forthwith, especially, if he make them but serviceable to the practice of piety, not for the instituting of Sects, although they deem the Quaker Sect the last, and that the Lord would now soon come to His Temple, forasmuch as the opinion concerning the Millennium is quite correct both amongst them and the Presbyterians, or Calvinists, both in Old and New England, as well as here, and even amongst the Quakers themselves a few years ago. It is consequently wrong to place all these into one category. The majority of them are just as worldly in their opinions, as any of the great divisions may be, and if all their members should be subjected to a particular examination on some points of Religion—the result would be, as amongst others —so many heads, so many opinions, as I have found out in mine own experience. (Here the letter ends abruptly).

VIGNETTE FROM TITLE PAGE OF THE "PARADISCHES WUNDERSPIEL," EPHRATA, 1761.

VIII.

LETTER TO HENRICH JOH. DEICHMAN, LONDON, ENGLAND.

Y health is still precarious, though considerably improved, God be praised. All of us are oftentimes exposed to severe temptations, yet our faithful Helper is ever near and often granteth us a splendid victory and bringeth it to pass, that we rule in the midst of our enemies. Much could be said on this subject: consider only, how Moses ruled over Pharaoh in Egypt, before gaining a complete victory, enabling him to sing his song of triumph at the Red Sea: consider, how David, who first was great in Babel, just as Moses in Egypt, ruled in the midst of Babel over Bel and Betraies, before he under David and Cyu (Cyrus?) assisted in the building of the temple: consider, how Christ ruled in the midst of death, before he rose. Think of Paul, a captive in Rome, David in the desert, etc. Thus also the new man ruleth in us, while yet he is surrounded by the old Adam, the sins, and death. At the sea of glass, he will sing the song of triumph of Moses and of the Lamb. Therefore we rejoice and are of good cheer, because we know, that the complete victory will finally be of God and the Lamb, and, therefore, ours. The new Adam within us, must, according to the prototype of the old one, sleep and be still, until his bride be fully built up and complete of his flesh and bone. O, how great will his joy and ours be, if . . . he now shall awake and recognize and name us as his own. Yea, when he shall have left his father and his mother, and shall cleave to us, because he is waiting therefor; why should we not wait a little for the consummation, because we shall be rewarded so richly therefor? How many have awakened love too soon, hindering thereby their growth

84

unto the fulness of their stature; how many have, with their strong spirit, striven too impetuously to attain something of the spiritual gifts of their inheritance, which they afterward squandered, and became poorer than they were at the beginning. Examples, such as these, we have in our days too, yea, even among our house-mates, who serve to teach us to endure in blessed waiting and resting in the will of God, until the destined end, meted out by His providence, arrive. O, how this watching and waiting is sweetened, in the mean time, for the humble, childlike souls that yearn for the holy will of their Father only, in so much that they would, indeed, wait forever, if their beloved Father would thus have it. And in this wise, they constantly become more humble and diminutive in their own estimation, in so much, that they finally deem themselves wholly unworthy of the revelation of their Friend and Bridegroom, whom they love so tenderly and for whom they yearn so eagerly; for the more they contemplate themselves, the more do they hate and despise their own self; but if they rise above themselves, they become entirely oblivious of their own self. And then their salvation is nearest, because they are farthest from their own self,   &c.

IX.

LETTER TO HESTER PALMER, AT FLUSHING, LONG ISLAND.

A. 1706 d. 25, Mayi.[1]

My dearly beloved in our Immanuel Jesus the Messiah:

The Son of God our Saviour.

EING presented lately with a letter of yours, directed to our beloved Friend M———— B————,[2] I found in the P. S. that the remembrance of mine was not yet slipt out of your Minde, insomuch that you desired to see a few lines from my hand, which Desire is an evident sign to me that the said remembrance is in Love and in the Truth.

Assure yourself that it is with no less Fervency on my Side, but I finde as yet a double wall between us, which indeed seems to stop the current of this firey love-dream of which no more at present, least we should embolden ourselves to break through before the time appointed by Him, who nourisheth the Woman in the Wilderness (Rev. 12, 14). And since our Discourse broke just as we was about this matter, Viz:—THE THREEFOLD WILDER-NESS STATE, I'll venture upon your Patience a few lines Concerning this subject, adding the Third State in the Wilderness, also having Confidence in your good Acceptance since you have in a manner bidden me to write and I finding no better Subject than to begin where we left it.

Of the first we did discourse somewhat, viz:—Of the Barren

---

[1] *Verbatim, et literatem.*

[2] The identity of this friend has not been discovered.

Wilderness, and as we was beginning the second, viz:—Of the Fruitfull Wilderness, we was interrupted.

The first hath a respect upon the Old Birth, like as Ye second upon the *New*. These two run parallel until the First dieth, and then the Second is set at Liberty. The first is begotten in Egypt, and then arriveth to its manhood, and being led out of Egypt falls and Dieth in the Wilderness. The Second is also begotten in Egypt but is educated, and arriveth to its manhood in the Wilderness, and after the death of the First enters Caanan. The First seeth indeed the stretched out Arm of God in Egypt as well as in the Wilderness, but murmurs, provokes and tempts God and limiteth the Holy one in Israel, alwais turning back with its Heart lusting after Egypt. The Second seeth God and its life is preserved, its face alwais turned Caananwarts and its Heart with Joshua and Caleb (Joshua signifieth Aid, Salvation, Conservation; Caleb, full of heart, courageous, undaunted, faithfull) stands faithfull and seeth Ye salvation of God, being filled with the fervent and only desire of attaining the same. The first is in continual fear of Death, and what he feareth cometh upon him (Num. 14, 28; Prov. 10, 24). The Second is undaunted and liveth (Num. 14, 30, 31) and puts his feet upon the necks of his enemies (Jos. 10, 24; Psal. 94, 13). The Second deriveth its origen from the First, and dying to this riseth and liveth in God: The First when He dyeth, liveth in the Second (This is a great Mystery and wants an Explanation else it may be misconstrued, but I hope you are no Stranger to it). The Second liveth under Moses as well as the First as long as Moses liveth (Gal. 4, 1; Rom. 7), but is hidd inward; by chance he is called the inward Man in the Tabernacle, from which He never departeth (Exod. 33, 11). But when Moses Dyeth the New Man, being arrived now to his Manhood, appears from his inward state outwardly to the Terror of his enemies (see of this coming forth Cant. 3, 6; and 8, 5) of Whose Land he taketh Possessión (Num. 27, 15; Deut. 3, 21–end). I will not draw the Parallism further, since a word to the Wise is enough. And since we have orally conferred of the First state, viz:—of Ye Barren

Wilderness, let us insist a little upon the Mystery of the Second. In which Fruitfull Wilderness we enjoy the leading Cloud by day, out of which so many drops of the heavenly Dew (Psal. 33, 3) as a Baptism of Grace upon us do fall. This is a Day of Joy and triumph, when the Holy Ghost moves and stirreth the waters in our Hearts so that this living spring diffuseth it self through the Eyes in a sweet and Joyfull Gush of Tears: O Thou blessed water-baptism, who would not desire to be Baptized with thee every day. But there followeth a night also upon this Day, wherein neverthe-less the Pillar of Fire is our Guide, refining us as Gold in the Furnace, which is the Baptism of Fire of Ye Son, and is indeed terrible to the old Birth, but bright and light to the New; for she learneth by this to be resigned and say 'Not my will, O Father! but Thine be done.' Thus our Tears are our Meat, yea, our Manna, not only by Day but also in the darkest Night (Psal. 42, 3; 80, 5). The most bitter Myrrh (which conditeth the old man in his Grave) hath the most sweetest Sweet hid in herself. For the Tree of the Cross and the Yoak of the Beloved doth but sweeten the bitter water of Affliction and sufferings in Mara (Exod. 15; Matt. 11). The darkest sorrow contains in herself the most inward Joy and Gladness (2 Cor. 6, 10). Darkness is like the Light (Psal. 139, 12). To dye is in this pleasant Wilderness to grow lively. Poverty maketh rich. Hunger is the most desirable Meat, and Thirst the most refreshing Nectar (Math. 5, 6). To be nothing is to be Deified (2 Pet. 1, 4). To have nothing is to enjoy all (2 Cor. 12, 10). To become weak is the greatest strength.

Disquietness is the surest Peace (2 Cor. 7, 10). No work no Pain doth tire, for the more we work the stronger we grow (Gen. 32, 24), and yet we do experimentally find that the greatest weak-ness hath the greatest strength hid in herself (Cant. 2, 5). Oh everblessed Wilderness thou rejoyceth and blossometh as a Rose! yea, thou blossometh abundantly and rejoyceth even with Joy and Singing. The glory of Libanon is given unto thee, the Excellency of Carmel and Sharon! In thee we see the Glory of our Lord, and the Excellency of our God! In thee our weak Hands are Strengthened and our feeble Knees confirmed (Esa. 35, 1). Who would not desire to be a Denizon in Thee? Who would not delight to trace thy Solitary and lonesom walks? O! ye Inhabitants of this happy desolation, bless and kiss that gentle hand of that Divine Sophia who at the first did so wittily allure you, when she intended to bring you into this Wilderness, for to speak to your Heart, in order to search and trie the same! Do not forsake her, untill she hath given you from hence your Possessions, and the hindermost Valley for the opening of your understanding (Hos. 2, 14, 15, according to the LXX Achor signifying hindermost, farthest, comp. Exod. 3, 1, Syrach 4, 17–28).

This Valley of Achor, or hindermost Cavity, leads me to the consideration of a Wilderness yet of a higher (further) degree than the Second, which it exceeds by so much as the second does the First. We may call it the WILDERNESS OF THE ELECT OF GOD, as being traced but by few, and none but peculiarly chosen Vessels of Honour and Glory.

I shall bring but four Instances for this, Two out of Ye Old and Two out of the New Test. The first is Moses, that great Prophet and mediator between God and the Israel, according to the Flesh, who, as the Acts 2, 7, give us to understand, had a Revelation that He should deliver Israel out of Egypt, whilst He was yet in the court of Pharao; which, as he would put in Execution, miscarried of the Enterprise through the fault of the People, whereupon he fled into the Wilderness, where he remained 40 years. What He did there is nowhere described, only that towards the end of the 40 years He led his Flock to the Backside (or rather to the hindermost or furthest) Desert. And there the Angel of the L(ord) appeared unto him out of a burning Bush, in order to send him in embassage to King Pharao. But so forward as Moses was at the first to go, when he had got only an Intimation or Manifestation or Revelation or Inspiration or Motion (or what we may call it) of what He now was to do, without any express Commission and Credentials (Viz. Miricales and

Signs). So backward was he now to go, when he got express orders and extraordinary Credentials, so that we may easily find what he had done during the 40 years in the Wilderness having the two extremes, viz., his Presumption and fervent Zeal at first in which he killed the Egyptian, and his great Humility and meekness at last when God would send him, which last is Symbolically typified by his leading his Sheep by Ye Backside or deepest of the Wilderness. Whereas formerly when his firy Quality was not yet thoroughly tinctured and Metamorphosed into the Lamlike nature, He led his flock, but, as it were, on the Brim and foreside of the Wilderness, of which I had more to say, but lest the Letter should exceed its bounds, I must hasten to the next Instance, which is Fleyah and runs into many things paralell to the first Witness. Read the history 1 Kings 6, 29. He was a very zealous and had slain the Priests of Baal, as Moses had the Egyptian. They did seek his life, as the Egyptians did Moses his. He made his escape and fled into the Wilderness as Moses did. Moses his 40 years was turned to him in 40 days, He came at last into the Hindermost Wilderness to the Mount of God Horeb, the very same where Moses saw the Vision, And here God appeared unto him, and gave him a gentle Reprimende as touching his Zeal and Presumtions. Shewing him withal, that the great and strong winde and the Earthquake and the Fire (wherein Elijah's his Ministry had consisted) did indeed go before the L(ord), but that the Lord did not dwell therein, but in the still ae thereall creating voice and that there were yet 7000 left besides him that had not bowed unto nor kissed Baal; though they were hid and unknown to him, and had not ministered publiquily with storming and quaking and burning Jealousy as he had done. Thereupon being Condemned to substitute another in his Room (viz: to edifie, whereas hitherto he had but destroyed), he was soon after taken up into Paradise, by the same element wherein he had ministered. This Eleijah leads to Ye first Wilderness in the New Testament, the Claus of the old John, the Precursor of the Messiah, who after his education was also in the Wilderness, till the day of his Shewing unto Israel in the Spirit and Power of

Eleijah, baptizing with water to Repentance, as the first Eleijah had baptized with Fier for Destruction. What he did in the Wilderness is not described, but by that what hath been said we may safely conclude that he was gratified there for his so great a Ministry. That God appeared also unto him there appeareth out of what he saith himself (Joh. 1, 33). He that sent me to Baptize the same said unto me. I will not draw the Parallelism any further, lest I should prove tedious at least. That like as the accorded of him who succeeded Eleijah, raised the dead man (2 Reg. 13, 21), so He who succeeded John, by his death became the Head, the Spring, the Principle and cause of Life and Resurrection unto all that believed in Him, both for Soul and Body. This is the last and greatest Witness I am to produce JESUS the Messiah of God, our God and Saviour, the centre of all, who also in likeness of the first Lawgiver Moses was 40 days (the 40 years of Moses being thus abridged) in the Wilderness and tempted there with all manner of Temptations (though without sin, wherein He hath the only Prerogative above all, Heb. 4, 15; 2, 28). The Scripture indeed maketh mention of his firey trials (1 Pet. 4, 12), But nowhere saith what they was or are. They cannot be described; it is only experience which can teach them best. The three temptations that happened at the End of the 40 days (Matt. 4) centre in this: *If He was the Son of God or Not!* which indeed hath more to say than is commonly supposed. The very Ground of the 'Christian Religion circling therein and is founded thereupon, as appears from Matt. 16, 16; Joh. 11, 27; 1 Joh. 4, 15; 5, 5; and is the greatest Stumbling block to the Jews (Joh. 19, 7) and to the Turks, the Latter believing that Jesus the Son of Mary (as they style him) is the word of God incarnate, and that he is anointed to the Holy Ghost above all the Prophets and above Mahomed, and that he is to be the Judge of the Quick and Dead and of Mahomed himself; but that He is the Son of God they cannot believe, for, say they, God is a Spirit and cannot beget a man for his Son, &c. And no wonder, this being a Mystery surpassing all humane and Angeelicall understanding; nor is it to be found out by the same, it depending solely from the Revelation of the Father, like as that of the Father depends from the Reception of the Son and M. K., is yet to answer the? Why Jesus being God of very God, became to be Man and died? The Prophets and Patriarchs have been tempted indeed with great Temptations, but none like this, none of the Nature of this, they being not capable of the same, as being the Sons of God through Faith in Him, who being God, was to be made Man (Exod. 3, 14, where it should have been interpreted: I Shall be, what I shall be, viz:—Man) as we through Faith in Him who was God and is made Man. But Jesus having past this firy ordeal, He received the Almightiness from his Father, whereof he made no bragging Ostentation, as Robbers make of their Pray, but humbled himself unto the death even the death of the Cross, styling himself at this side of the Grave only the son of Man (or mankind, the Greek word denoting both the Sexes) though He was the son of God: Wherefore God also by the Resurrection from the Dead powerfully declared him to be his Son (Rom. 1, 4; Psal. 2. Act.) exalting him above all, Lord over all worlds, visible and invisible, this and that which is to come (Eph. 1, 2; Phil. 2, 6–11).

To these four I will add two more out of the Scripture, passing by the rest (Heb. 11, 38). This first is *David,* that man after God's own Heart, who was 10 years in the Wilderness and exercised in continual Sufferings and Sorrows (as his Psalms bear witness) before He was installed in the Kingdom, to which He was chosen and annointed so many years before. The second is that great Apostle of the Gentiles *Paul,* who abided seven years in the Deserts of Arabia (Gal. 1, 17, and as the antient Church Records bear witness), before he went out for the Conversion of the Gentiles. I could produce a whole Cloud of such chosen Vessels out of the antient Records of the first Christians, who beeing prepared in the Wild's some for 10, some for 20, some for 40 years, after their coming forth converted whole Cities, wrought signs and Miracles, was to their Disciples as living Oracles, as the mouth of God through whom he fed and guided them, but having exceeded the limits of a letter allready, I must stop the Vein which so liberally would diffuse it self; I hope what hath been said manifested to the full, that God hath prepared alwais his most eminent Instruments in the Wilderness.

When we consider now with a serious introversion of our minds those Three states of the Wild's, we shall find That there is no entring into the first Wild's without a going out of Spiritual Egypt; and so consequently no entring into the second without passing the first; And so on, no entring into the Third without passing the second state.

We shall find in the next place, that like as there is a long Struggling and Groaning under the Egyptian Burdens before the delivery from the same ensueth, So there is a long contest between the first and second Birth in their Wilderness-Station before the Second is set at perfect Liberty and made ready to enter and possess Caanan: But how long the Parallelism of the second and third state may run together, and where the Borders of each meet together or if there be any Borders at all, I'll leave to higher graduated Souls than mine is to enquire; by it to speak my mind: me thinks the Childhood and Manhood may both well consist with the second state, and one may arrive to the manhood in Christ without ever entering the Third Station, this being only for some chosen Vessels for a peculiar administration which requires also peculiar and extraordinary Qualifications and Endowments, which they are to acquire and make trial of in this Third Station before they appear and show themselves to the Israel of God. So that every one that is to enter the Third must of necessity be acquainted with the second and first. But not every one that hath entered the Second and after he is even with the first must also enter the Third Station.

By the consideration of the Third State we shall find what a wighty thing it is to appear and to show oneself to the Israel of God, as immediately called chosen and sent by the Lord. Such a being made, as Paul saith (1 Cor. 4, 9) a Spectacle to the World and to Angels and to Men. And what good reason Moses had to resist so hard when he was sent, whom God having heard the crey and Prayers of his People, did force as it were and thrust or cast

forth (see Matt. 11, 38) where it should have been thurst or ——
forth instead of sent forth). And what a great presumption it is,
on the other Hand, to go forth without being thus duly prepared
beforehand. For though such may have inspirations, Revelations,
Motions and the like Extraordinary Favours; yea, may have arrived
at the very Manhood in Christ (which truly is a high attainment),
yet they will effect and build nothing, but only (if they do any thing
at all) destroy, as we see in the instances of Moses and Elias,
before they had been in that Wild's. Yea, there is no small Danger
of loosing themselves and to bruise and grind that good seed, which
was not designed for Meat but for increase, not for to be sent forth
but to be kept in an honest and Good Heart. (Luc. ——). Such
are indeed with Child, they are in pain, but (as the common
Translation saith, Esa. 26, 28, and as the common experience
wittnesseth to be so) they bring forth as it were but Winde, they
make no deliverance in the earth, neither do the Inhabitants of the
World fall; Whereas if they was duly prepared and had stood the
firey ordeal it would fare with them, not as with the common, but
as the Translation the first Christians made use of hath it: Through
thy Tears Lord we have conceived and have been in Pain of Birth,
and have brought forth the Spirit of Salvation, which Salvation we
have wrought on Earth; we shall not fall, but all that dwell on
Earth shall fall.

I had many Considerations more to add, as also what the Wilderness it self is in each of these States, having spoken only of some
of the Inhabitants thereof and of some of their Qualities and
Circumstances, and this rather under a veil and, as it were, but
glancing at the Marrow and Substance. Nor have I counted the
number of the Wilderness-Time, but touched only the root thereof,
which is 40 Sun-Days for the New Birth and 42 Moons or Nights
for the Old (which last I have not so much as mentioned).
Neither have I measured from the Red-Sea of the Old Birth to the
Jordan of the New, and a hundred such things more. But my
beloved and esteemed Friend! this was to write a Volume and not
a Letter, And I begin allmost to fear that I have ventured too much

John A. *[handwritten inscription]*

A
SHORT, EASY,
AND
COMPREHENSIVE
METHOD
OF
PRAYER.

Translated from the German.
and published for a farther *Promotion, Knowledge and Benefit* of Inward Prayer,

By a Lover of Internal Devotion.

PHILADELPHIA,
Printed by Henry Miller, in Second-street, next to the Corner of Race-street.
M.DCC.LXI.

A
SHORT, EASY,
AND
COMPREHENSIVE
METHOD
OF
PRAYER.

Translated from the German.
And published for a farther *Promotion, Knowledge and Benefit* of Inward Prayer.

By a Lover of Internal Devotion.

The Second Edition with Addition.

GERMANTOWN,
Printed by *Christopher Sower.*
M.DCC.LXIII.

upon your Patience this first time, not considering also the wall between us. Oh! that we may behold our Beloved alwais, standing behind our Wall, looking forth att the Window, shewing himself thorow the Lattesse, saying Rise up my Love, my fair one and come away (Cant. 29, 10). To whose Love-embraces leaving you, I remain,

Your sincere, though unworthy Friend,

J. K.

ROCKSBORROW, 1706, d. 25, Maji.
  For Hesther Pallmer,
    in Long-Island in Flushing.

X.

KELPIUS'S "METHOD OF PRAYER."

OW concerned Magister Kelpius was for the spiritual welfare of the German settlers in Penn's Colony on the Delaware, where every effort was made by the Quakers to incorporate the Germans in their fold, is shown by the compilation by Kelpius of a little prayer book of 32 pages, six inches by 3½ inches. The title of this brochure was „Eine Kurtze und Begreifflige anleitung zum stillen Gebet."

No copy of the original edition, so far as known, has come down to us. It is said to have been printed by Reynier Jansen, about the year 1700, and was the first German devotional book to be printed in the west-

Kurtzer

Begriff

oder leichtes

Mittel

zu beten,

oder mit GOtt zu reden.

Demnach das innere Gebät ein so wichtiger Punct ist, daß man dasselbe das eintzige Mittel nennen kan, zu der Vollkommenheit in diesem Leben zugelangen, und die lautere uninteressirte Liebe in unsern Hertzen anzurichten: und da alle Christen (welche solche in der That seyn wollen) zu diesem Stand der lautern Liebe und Vollkommenheit beruffen sind, und denenselben kraft dieses Rufs die nöthige Gnade dargereichet wird, um solchen Stand zu erreichen: so schickt sich dieses innere Gebet für allerley Personen, ja so gar auch für die allersimpelste und allerdumste Leute, als welche solcherley Art des Gebets fähig sind, und es verrichten können.

Es bringt uns dasselbe am allerbaldigsten zu der Vereinigung und zu der Einförmigkeit des

A   Willens

ern world, nor is it known whether this was printed with German or Latin type.[1]

A second German edition was printed by Franklin and Armbruster in 1756, of which the only known copy is in the collection of the writer. There evidently was no general title page; the printers and date are known from the advertisements in the local paper.

A facsimile of the first page with its half title „Kurzer Begriff oder leichtes Mittel zu Beten oder mit Gott zu reden," is shown upon the opposite page, following is Dr. Christopher Witt's translation of the text:

> " For as much as internal Prayer is so
> Weighty a Point, that one may call
> it the only means to attain to Per-
> fection in this Life, and to kindle the Pure
> and disinterested Love in our Heart's; and
> as all Christians (who will indeed be such)
> are Called to this State of pure Love and per-
> fection, and will, by the power of this call
> have the necessary Grace offered to them
> to attain such a State. So this inward
> prayer suits all persons, even the most
> Simple and ignorant, who are also capable of
> performing this Order or Manner of prayer.
>   This brings us soonest to the Union with
> and Conformity to the Will of God! "

Dr. Christopher Witt[2] who translated this pamphlet into English was an English physician and mystic, who joined the mystical community on the Wissahickon in the

---

[1] *Cf.* " German Pietists in Provincial Pennsylvania," Phila., Kelpius, 1895, p. 102.

[2] *Ibid.*

year 1704, and died in 1765 at the advanced age of ninety years, being the last survivor of the Kelpius community on the Wissahickon.

Dr. Witt's English translation was first printed by Henry Miller, the German printer of Philadelphia, in the year 1761, whose establishment was on Second Street next to the corner of Race Street. Dr. Witt gave a copy of this edition to Christian Lehman of Germantown, who had been one of his students, who made the following notes upon the back of the title and last page of his copy, viz. :[3]

Reverse of Title:

Christian Lehman, Favore, Christophori, De Witt, Natus, 10th November 1675 in Wiltshire in England. Given xbr: 5th A° Dom. 1763, Denatus at Germantown, January 30th, A° Dom 1765 Buried February 1st 1765, Etatis Sue 89 years 2 months 20 days Natus 10th Novembr A. D. 1675.

On last page:

The foregoing was originally composed in the German Tongue by John Kelpius a German and was Translated into English by Christopher Witt who died January 30th 1765, aged 89 yrs 2 mo. 20 days.

Dr. Witt was buried in the Warner burying ground on the hill top back of the Warner house, at the corner of the Main and High Street, locally known as "Spook hill."[4] A part of this ground is now covered by the chancel of St. Michael's P. E. Church, under the floor of which rest his remains.

Two years later, 1763, a second edition of the English version of Kelpius's pamphlet was published at German-

---

[3] For full account of Dr. Witt, *cf. ibid.*, pp. 402–418.

[4] *Cf.* pp. 419–430.

THE PENNSYLVANIA-GERMAN SOCIETY.

ST. MICHAEL'S P. E. CHURCH.

Christian Lehman

Favor

' Let us afcend the Mountain with Jefus Chrift; let us pray as he has prayed; let us contemplate, let us love; fo fhall we perform God's prayer.

O divine Jefus! I join with thee in the Prayer which thou haft in Solitude by Night prayed, in this prayer of God; grant that we may perform no other Prayer.

O God! fend this internal Spirit over the whole Earth; fo will it be anew created, Let this Spirit reft on the Waters of thy ufual and wonted Grace, which thou offereft to all Men; fo will it diftribute an overflowing Fruitfulnefs.

O give us new Hearts.
Amen, O Jefus!

Christophoro DeWitt

Natus 10th November 1675 in Wiltshire in England,

Given Xbr: 5 th St Dom,

1769

Denatus at Germantown January 30th Ao Dom: 1765
Burd Febertuary 1st 1765

Ætatis sue 8 yrs 3 m3 & Days.

Natus 10th Novembr Ao 1675:

The foregoing was original Compos'd or by the German Tongue by John Kelpius a German & Duo Frans: lated into English by Christopher Witt who died January 30th 1765 aged 89.47. 2 M3. 20 Days.

THE

FACSIMILE OF INSCRIPTION ON REVERSE OF TITLE, AND UPON LAST PAGE OF CHRISTIAN LEHMAN'S KELPIUS PRAYER BOOK.

town by Christopher Sower, as the title states, "The Second edition with addition." No copy with any additional matter has thus far been found. The copy printed by Sower in the Historical Society is merely a reprint of the Miller edition of 1761.

Facsimiles of title pages of both English editions are shown upon the opposite page. The originals are in the Historical Society of Pennsylvania.

Magister Johannes Kelpius was small of stature, slight in frame, and suffered from an affection or paralysis of the left eyelid; he was of a frail constitution, which soon broke down under frugal fare and abstemious habits and the extremes of our variable climate.

Kelpius died in the year 1708, at the early age of thirty-five. He was buried with the rites of the Mystical community at sunset by his brethren. His resting place is not known.

JULIUS F. SACHSE.

September 20, 1916.

Metalmark Books is a joint imprint of The Pennsylvania State University Press and the Office of Digital Scholarly Publishing at The Pennsylvania State University Libraries. The facsimile editions published under this imprint are reproductions of out-of-print, public domain works that hold a significant place in Pennsylvania's rich literary and cultural past. Metalmark editions are primarily reproduced from the University Libraries' extensive Pennsylvania collections and in cooperation with other state libraries. These volumes are available to the public for viewing online and can be ordered as print-on-demand paperbacks.

LIBRARY OF CONGRESS CATALOGING-IN-PUBLICATION DATA

Kelpius, John, 1667?–1708.
The diarium of Magister Johannes Kelpius / Johannes Kelpius ; translated with annotations by Julius Friedrich Sachse.
p.   cm.
Originally published: Lancaster, Pa. : Press of the New Era Print. Co., 1917.
Summary: "An English translation, originally published by the Pennsylvania German Society in 1917, of the diary of radical German Pietist Johannes Kelpius (1667–1708). Includes facsimile pages of his prayer book A Short, Easy, and Comprehensive Method of Prayer"—Provided by publisher.
ISBN 978-0-271-05646-3 (pbk. : alk. paper)
1. Kelpius, John, 1667?–1708—Diaries.
2. Pietists—Diaries.
I. Sachse, Julius Friedrich, 1842–1919.
II. Title.
BR1653.K45A3 2012
280'.4092—dc23
[B]
2012023591

Printed in the United States of America
Reprinted by The Pennsylvania State University Press, 2012
University Park, PA 16802-1003